Birds of a Feather

We love the outdoors! More great titles from Islandport Press.

Backtrack
By V. Paul Reynolds

This Cider Still Tastes Funny!
By John Ford Sr.

Suddenly, the Cider Didn't Taste So Good!
By John Ford Sr.

Tales from Misery Ridge
By Paul Fournier

Where Cool Waters Flow
By Randy Spencer

My Life in the Maine Woods
By Annette Jackson

Nine Mile Bridge
By Helen Hamlin

These and other books are available at:
www.islandportpress.com.

Islandport Press is a dynamic, award-winning publisher dedicated to stories rooted in the essence and sensibilities of New England. We strive to capture and explore the grit, beauty, and infectious spirit of the regional by telling tales, real and imagined, that can be appreciated in many forms by readers, dreamers, and adventurers everywhere.

Birds of a Feather

Paul Fournier

ISLANDPORT PRESS

Islandport Press
P.O. Box 10
247 Portland Street
Yarmouth, Maine 04096
www.islandportpress.com
books@islandportpress.com

ISBN: 978-1-939017-04-8
Library of Congress Card Number: 2013930187

Dean L. Lunt, publisher
Book jacket design, Karen F. Hoots, Hoots Design
Book design, Michelle A. Lunt
Cover photo by Paul Fournier; courtesy Maine State Museum

To My Siblings:
Felix, Eugene and Pamela
Dearly Departed: Rene and Lila

Table of Contents

About the Author

For Paul Fournier, the Maine outdoors was both home and office, inspiration and mission.

One could say the veteran Maine guide, journalist, bush pilot, professional photographer, and filmmaker was both a self-made man and a lucky one. Eager to learn skills by any means, he seized new challenges as they arose and fashioned a career that he loved.

The widely published Fournier shares his adventures in his award-winning *Tales from Misery Ridge* and this newest volume, *Birds of a Feather*.

Fournier grew up during the Great Depression in Jay, Maine, a paper mill town. As a young teen he distinguished himself for skipping school, perhaps even setting a record. At fourteen he began working, and at sixteen he started unloading boxcars of pulpwood on the night shift at the mill for sixty-five cents an hour.

But one teacher got him interested in reading and geography, a gift that set him on a lifelong path that combined working in the outdoors and documenting his experiences. At fifteen, outfitted with a canoe, he explored bogs and ponds as much as he could, and read everything he could get his hands on. The local game warden took notice, and at eighteen Fournier became a Registered Maine Guide, taking guests at a camp on Richardson Lake on fishing trips. "We caught our limit almost every day," he said.

Paul Fournier poling a canoe up Allagash Stream while guiding a party.

He married his first wife, Anita Giasson, a waitress he met at the camp, in 1950. The Korean War intervened, and Fournier became an instructor for the Air Force.

In 1955, after he was discharged, the newlyweds bought a sporting camp on a remote lake, an outpost with just a few cabins and boats. Fournier guided trips in earnest, clearing brush and building tent platforms in his spare time. Business boomed at Brassua Lake Camps & Campground, one of the first commercial campgrounds in Maine. During the same period, Fournier worked as a bush pilot for Dick Folsom on Moosehead Lake, taking wealthy clients, river drivers, and foresters wherever they needed to go.

In the winters, when business was slow, Fournier started writing. "I had incredible luck for someone like me, a dropout at sixteen," he said. He took a job at a newspaper in Lewiston.

Some of his stories were picked up by the Associated Press, and he eventually became sports editor for the *Bath Daily Times*.

In his spare time, Fournier started covering the Maine coast and fishing industry. "I wrote all kinds of material about the waterways of Maine," he said. One could argue he was Maine's first environmental writer.

In 1967, Fournier was offered a job as publicity officer for the Maine Department of Marine Resources. When the department wanted to make films about new fishing and safety techniques, Fournier became its go-to man.

"That's been the story of my life. I jumped into things I didn't know anything about," Fournier recalled with a chuckle.

Soon thereafter, an acquaintance asked him to make instructional films for a ski area, which led to more ski films and promotions for the state economic development department. When that office eventually shut down, Fournier—equipped with not only excellent writing skills, but also film production experience and footage—started his own company. He created several Maine film segments for national television.

In 1980, the Maine Department of Inland Fisheries and Wildlife offered him a job as public information officer, which is how Fournier closed out his formal career. It was a job he called "the best in the world."

He retired in 1996, and moved to Connecticut with his second wife, Lorraine. "I've been lucky to have two wonderful marriages," he said.

Fournier passed away in August, 2013, just days after completing the final edits for *Birds of a Feather*. *Birds* and *Tales from Misery Ridge*, his first book, bring together a lifetime of engaging observations and tales.

Indeed, as eyewitness to and documentarian for much of the Maine outdoors and sports world for more than fifty years, Fournier now stands as one of Maine's premier outdoor historians.

Part 1:
On Land

1

Moose Without Borders

How 9/11 Changed the Hunt for Border-Crossing Poachers

FOR MANY YEARS, Quebec hunters killed and registered a large number of moose in the small communities scattered along the Canadian border with Maine.

This was strange because moose are rare in that southern part of the province. The land has been settled and cultivated for many generations. It's farmland, not moose habitat. So where did the moose come from? Maine, of course. They were literally lured to the Canadians' gun sights.

The land on the Maine side of the boundary is owned by large timber and paper companies, used as woodlands to supply mills on both sides of the border. Their forest-management practices over the years have created a utopian habitat for moose.

I received a firsthand introduction to this some years ago when I was invited by game warden Lieutenant Gray Morrison to go along with wardens "working" the Canadian moose hunt. For years Maine wardens, aware of the Canadians' coveting of Maine moose, patrolled the areas near the border to prevent Canadians from coming across to poach moose. Some Canadians did so successfully for years. Many simply tried to entice the Maine moose into crossing the border. Once a moose steps over the line it instantly becomes Canadian, and fair game.

In company with wardens Charley Davis and Morrison, I took a canoe ride down the West Branch of the St. John River, which forms the border between the two countries for many miles. Every few hundred yards, sometimes closer, we saw elaborate tree houses—no mere tree stands here—and all were occupied by from one to several hunters. All were facing east— into Maine.

We were "undercover" (i.e., wearing hunter garb), but I doubt if we were fooling these guys. We passed dozens of these tree houses. I never got into one, but I was told that some were comfortably tricked out, with camp stoves, old chairs and sofas, even bunks for overnighting. I wouldn't be surprised if some had TVs. (And some were practically in farmers' backyards.)

What these guys were doing, of course, was calling moose— trying to lure them into crossing over into Canada to be shot. Hunters know that bull moose, caught in the madness of the rut, can be enticed to close range with some clever calling to imitate the sounds of a receptive female, or the challenge of a rival bull. Some of these Canadians were adept at the practice. Some used traditional horns made of birch bark, or electronic callers; others used a large coffee can. With a hole punched through the bottom of the can and a well-rosined string or leather thong attached to it. When pulled, the string emits a sound that many hunters—and they hope some bull moose— think closely imitates the sound of a cow moose. It sometimes works.

As long as the Canadians stayed on their side of the border in the tree houses, they were perfectly legal. But for years Maine wardens had waged a campaign against people who slipped across the largely unguarded border to shoot moose on the Maine side and bring them back to Canada. One large ring of market hunters was broken up in the 1980s in a joint operation by Maine and Quebec wardens. It was alleged they were killing moose in Maine, hauling the meat across, hidden among the loads of logging trucks that cross into Canada daily. (Huge sawmills are located in towns in Quebec, dependent on the nearby Maine forest for their raw material.) Once across the border, the hunters would sell the meat to exclusive restaurants in Montreal and Quebec City that specialize in wild game dinners.

In one instance, Maine biologists had been monitoring a radio-collared moose by air when it suddenly disappeared. On a flight to western Maine, a faint signal was received from that collar transmitter. It was pulsing in "dead mode." (If a collar stops moving, as when an animal dies, its signal changes.) It became apparent the signal was coming from across the border in Quebec.

Working in conjunction with Canadian wardens, and with a warden plane circling overhead, they narrowed the source of the signal to a farmer's barn, where they found the "dead" collar hanging on a nail. The farmer, not knowing its signal capabilities, had hung it up as a self-incriminating "trophy."

During my canoe trip down the St. John with the wardens, we spotted a number of moose paunches, where successful hunters had gutted their animals and dumped the innards in the river.

Later that day I met warden pilot Dana Toothaker. We flew over miles of the border—a narrow, cleared strip through the woods—and found dozens more tree houses, all manned. Flying at low altitude, we could occasionally see a hunter aim his rifle up at us, apparently checking us out with his rifle scope. I kept hoping that none, annoyed at our presence, would pull the trigger.

Since 9/11, Maine–Canada border hunting has declined— victim, strangely enough, to the fallout from that national tragedy. According to Roger Guay, retired commanding officer of the Moosehead area regional warden headquarters (which has jurisdiction over much of the western Maine–Quebec boundary region), stepped-up surveillance and patrols by the US Border Patrol, including frequent helicopter overflights and numerous satellite-linked sensors placed along the boundary, proved a major deterrent to moose-seeking forays into Maine. Canadians discovered in the midst of illegal incursions face fines of five thousand dollars, plus confiscation of vehicles and equipment.

Said Guay: "It's relieved our Maine wardens of a big burden, making it possible to concentrate more of our efforts on our own problems."

2

Shadows in the Woods

Do Cougars Roam in Maine?

WHAT WERE WE, TWO EMPLOYEES of the state fish and wildlife department, doing skulking in a hot, smelly chicken barn on a warm, late-summer day when we could have been in our air-conditioned offices? We were hunting. Cougar hunting. Not with guns, but with binoculars and long-lensed cameras.

With me on the second floor of this empty building formerly used for raising poultry was regional wildlife biologist Gene Dumont. For months, Gene's office had been receiving reports of cougar sightings in the area around Bristol, on the coastal peninsula south of Damariscotta. The Maine Department of Inland Fisheries and Wildlife (IF&W) receives dozens of reports of such sightings each year, and makes attempts to track them down. Usually, they turn out to be mistaken identities: coyotes, dogs, fishers. But there was something about these persistent sighting reports that required more than just casual interest on our part.

The woman who lived in the farmhouse by the chicken barn reported to Gene that she had seen this animal several days in a row, always following the same routine: It would approach a large pine tree across the road from her house, climb into the tree, and lie there on a branch for extended periods of time. She said once it even showed up when she and another woman were sitting on the lawn, paying them no attention.

To the biologist, this seemed like the ideal opportunity to prove or disprove once and for all: Are there really cougars in Maine? He invited me to bring my cameras, and we decided the best location from which to hide and watch without being observed by the big cat was the stinky barn.

And of course, despite our long, sweaty hours inhaling the rank mustiness of that barn, the cat chose not to show up that day. Later, Gene climbed up the pine tree and found several hairs caught in the bark where the animal had lain. Analysis at a lab confirmed that they were indeed feline hairs, but could not conclusively identify them as cougar.

Cougars (also called panthers, pumas, mountain lions, catamounts [cat of the mountains], painters, and Indian Devils) have officially been extinct in the eastern United States since at least the 1920s or '30s, yet reports of sightings occur dozens of times each year. Some are hard to dispel.

⊰⊱⋇⊰⊱

I first began hearing reports of cougar sightings back in the 1950s when I was living at Brassua Lake. One evening three of our "sports" had been driving the road from Jackman to our camps. They arrived late in the evening, brimming with excitement. At the time, the Jackman road was a narrow gravel path, running over twenty miles through uninhabited wilderness. These guys excitedly related to me that they had seen a mountain lion cross the road near Smiley Hill. They had had a good view of it in the car headlights, and described it in

8

illustration by Mark McCullough

Sketch of hunting cougar

minute detail: the rounded face, tawny color, black-tipped tail.
They were pretty darned convincing; I was half-sold. Strange,
though, that these guys "from away" (New York, as I recall)
were the only ones I'd ever heard of that had seen a lion in the
area. I had frequently driven that road, and the local residents
drove it routinely. Guys were always in the woods, logging,
hunting, traveling to and from work, etc. None had ever
reported seeing a big cat. Yet these three, on their once-a-year
drive, had.

Convincing though they may have been, they lost their
credibility with me when, the very next day, they drove the few
miles from my camps to Rockwood—and on the way, spotted

a second cougar! That was simply too much. They seemed perfectly sober, and hallucinatory drugs were unknown to the area at the time, so I don't know what they thought they saw. Nonetheless, my willingness to believe was shattered, and my skepticism level has been elevated ever since.

Accounts of a second series of cougar sightings began reaching me after I'd sold the camps and moved to the coastal Maine area when I took the job as sports editor of the *Bath Daily Times* (now the *Times Record*). I began writing a lot about outdoors stuff (my first love), and this began attracting calls and visits from people with similar interests.

One person who became the most frequent of these was a gentleman from the area who began dropping into my office every few weeks for lengthy chats (sometimes too lengthy, when I was up against printing deadlines). But always, he had some new, exciting news—especially relating to reported sightings of cougars, or of their signs. I quoted him a time or two, which only served to encourage him. Jim (not his real name, for reasons evident later) was a well-educated man who had traveled widely in his profession and was extremely well-spoken. He exuded credibility.

But though he talked a good game, he never seemed to come up with anything tangible. Time after time he would show up with breathtaking tales of surefire evidence of the presence of cougars—tracks, scats, kills, etc. He was always on the verge of going out to meet the people who had made these discoveries (he was plugged in to an apparent network of cougar-sighters), and, as soon as he had confirmed the evidence, he would be sure to call me so I could go with him with a camera to document the finding and interview the finders.

Somehow, this never seemed to happen. He would drop out of sight for a few weeks. When he showed up again, he always had a new, wonderfully positive sighting to report. But when I asked about the previous sure-thing report, he would become evasive, as if he'd completely forgotten about it. I soon learned to consider his visits as just that: visits with a pleasant fellow.

Of course, during the years I was at IF&W, I heard numerous reports of sightings. The folks who reported these were adamantly positive of what they had seen. Cougars. They were dogmatic in their belief, even though most seemed to be amateur observers: housewives, children, "city people" from away. Seldom were they seasoned woodsmen, trappers, guides, game wardens—the people who spend much of their lives in the woods.

But there was an exception or two.

One of the most credible sightings that came my way happened in the Allagash Wilderness Waterway State Park. A couple of park rangers were in a boat traveling in the Thoroughfare, a long, narrow stretch of water connecting Churchill and Eagle lakes. The water level was down, exposing a narrow area of clear space between the water and the brush. Suddenly they spotted down near the water a sizable brown animal which both instantly were convinced was a cougar. On their approach the animal suddenly turned and dashed for the brush. One of the men had a video camera and snatched a quick shot of the animal just as it disappeared into the bushes.

At last, here was proof positive of the existence of cougar in Maine!

I was told the video was being transported to me so we could examine it in my video lab. I awaited it with, as they say, bated breath.

The video arrived a few days later. A group of us—including senior biologists, wardens, and the just plain curious—gathered in the video studio to examine the film. This was in the days of VHS half-inch videotape—much lower in quality than today's digital. The fellow's camera had apparently been one of lower quality, as well. It had been shot under poor light conditions, from a rocky boat, by an unsteady hand. And it was just the briefest of shots, a few frames only. It was blurry, shaky, grainy, and poorly focused (no discredit to the shooter; best he could do under the circumstances).

The studio was equipped to run the video at various speeds, including stop-motion for frame-by-frame examination. We ran it over and over, at every possible speed, and examined each frame. Sure, we saw a sizable, dark brown animal (dark perhaps because it was wet) dashing madly for the brush. Some thought they could distinguish the long, thin tail, others could not. There was one frame where, just as the animal ducked into cover, it did indeed look like there was a tail lashing sideways. But perhaps not. Unfortunately, it was not convincing. It was impossible to get a positive, conclusive identification from the footage.

<hr/>

The subspecies known as eastern cougar, *Felis concolor couguar*, is similar to but separate from the western cougar, *Felis concolor missoulensis*. While the western and Florida panthers are not only holding their own but increasing in numbers and range, the eastern cougar remains officially extinct as it has for nearly a century. Oh, scientists admit there have been and probably still are a few cougars loose in Maine, but they insist these are not eastern cougars. They are cats that have been deliberately released, or escaped, from captivity as pets. And they are mainly South American cougars, which are apparently easily obtained and favored in the pet trade. Exact numbers are unknown, but it is estimated there are many caged cougars in Maine. Gene Dumont believed the Bristol cougar that kept visiting the farmer's wife was of this origin.

There is, reportedly, one small population of cougars close to Maine. Dr. Bruce Wright of New Brunswick has written widely about what he says is a remnant population of cougars in that province. In a pamphlet released by the Minister of the Environment Information, Canada, Wright has written that ". . . the eastern cougar, once thought extinct, is managing to breed . . . It is not a hazard to man's interests in any way in the large, unsettled areas of this province."

Isn't it possible that cougars so close by would occasionally visit Maine? Very likely. The border between the two is primarily the St. Croix River. It could be easily crossed, especially in times of low water, or in winter over the frozen ice. In fact, Washington County in eastern Maine accounts for many of the reported cougar sightings. Could they be Canadian aliens?

The cougar once ranged widely throughout both North and South America, wherever its chief prey, deer, were found. The early European settlers began waging war on it soon after arrival, as it attacked their livestock, and, occasionally, people themselves, according to some reports.

In Maine, I'm aware of only one such reported attack on a human.

In his elder years Silvanus Poor, one of the earliest settlers in the area of Andover in western Maine, was interviewed by his niece, Agnes Blake Poor. He described the incident as follows: Two trappers on the Magalloway River (in the remote corner of Maine where the borders of New Hampshire and Canada meet) separated to check their trap-sets. When one failed to return, a search was started, "following his tracks in the new-fallen snow," said Mr. Poor. "They soon found the tracks of some large creature of the cat kind that appeared to be following him, and then the spot where he had been killed and almost eaten up, supposed to be a catamount by the tracks."

Another hunter-trapper who operated long traplines for many years in much the same area was J. (Joshua) G. (Gross) Rich. In the mid- to late-1800s, the noted woodsman wrote widely about his life in the outdoor magazines of the day. J. G. was not known for modesty. He boasted, "I have hunted over twenty years of my life as a profession, in the wilds of northern Maine. I hunted alone and camped alone many years; have followed hunting lines sixty-five miles long with traps all the way, which took all the week days—I did not hunt on Sundays—through the season. I have killed seventy-three black bears, between fifty and sixty moose, and several hundred Canada lynx, besides caribou, red deer, otters, fishes [sic], fox, mink, martin [sic], and other game. I trapped forty-nine lynx in one season."

Rich even gives a breathless account of being attacked by a lynx, which he single-handedly captured live, being thoroughly scratched up in the process. But curiously, not a word about a cougar, which apparently had already been exterminated in the area.

Early on, settlers attacked the catamount (as it was popularly called) with guns, dogs, and traps. For many years, bounties of up to fifty dollars were paid for killed cougars. And concurrently, its ancient habitat was being altered into farmlands and settlements. It has never recovered.

One now-legendary hunter-trapper from recent times might well have rivaled J. G. Rich for wilderness experience. Al Nugent of Chamberlain Lake, in the Allagash Wilderness region of northern Maine, ran long traplines through that region before roads reached it. He killed many animals over the years, including Canada lynx, bobcats, and bears. During the years I knew him, although he enjoyed talking about his experiences, I never recall him mentioning cougars. That country (unlike now) was overrun with deer, the cougar's main prey. If they were to be found anywhere, it seems it would have been here.

For many years it was considered great sport in Maine to hunt bobcats with dogs; it was a bit lucrative, too, as a bounty was being paid on the cats. Also, game wardens routinely went out to deer-wintering areas on snowshoes with dogs to shoot deer-killing bobcats. I recall during the 1950s when wardens like Norman Harriman, Wally Barron, and others would snowshoe into the big deer yard (wintering area) along Churchill Stream, just over Misery Ridge from my camps, with hunting dogs to shoot deer-killing bobcats. I never heard them mention cougars. (That deer yard, along with numerous others, no longer exists, cut over for its wealth of lumber. A Maine wildlife biologist once told me: "Every time you see a truckload of cedar posts or fencing go down I-95 out of state, there goes another deer yard!")

Little wonder that the Maine deer population, following several severe deep-snow winters, is decimated over much of northern and eastern Maine. Cougars, if they did try to exist here, would find slim pickings.

Another seemingly great source, it seems, would be the state wildlife biologists, who routinely make frequent visits to survey deer yards in their regions. In winter, they maintain Winter Severity Index stations in known deer yards, where several times a week they retrieve data regarding high and low temperatures, measure snow depths, and check on the condition of available browse and deer health conditions. While with the Department, I often went along with guys like deer biologist Gerry Lavigne and Bill Noble of the Greenville Regional Office to film these activities. I never saw, nor did these guys ever mention, any sign of cougars in these "yards" (actually, some cover square miles of territory), which, since they concentrated deer, would seem the most logical place for cougars to be found.

What is the official opinion on the status of cougars in Maine?

There is today no more esteemed and respected scientist with knowledge of the subject than Dr. Mark McCollough, endangered species specialist with the US Fish and Wildlife Service, stationed near Old Town. Mark's credentials are without peer. He has spent time in the West studying cougars—their habits, tracks, scats, etc. He is no ivory-tower academic.

He has an infectious sense of humor and is fast with the quips. Recently while addressing a public group, he said of the frequent reports of cougars that they were UFOs: "Unidentified Feline Objects."

He told the same audience that "extraordinary claims require extraordinary evidence. Ninety to ninety-five percent of reports of cougar sightings are the mistaken identification of other species of wildlife."

This was an unwelcome statement to the dozens of folks who adamantly believe they have, indeed, seen cougars. The bloggers had a field day.

In 2012 McCollough undertook a review of the eastern cougar to report to his scientific peers. His comments: "During a three-year period, USFWS biologists [including McCollough] reviewed all the available US and Canadian literature and held discussions with cougar groups, people who have seen cougars in the wild, geneticists, State agency biologists, Canadian Wildlife Service biologists, and endangered species biologists (from several eastern regions). . . . Biologists reviewed 573 comments received in response to a request for information. They also requested information from the 21 states within the historical range of the eastern cougar. No evidence supports the existence of an eastern cougar population."

The report further states: "We analyzed the best available information and concluded the eastern cougar no longer exists. We believe the subspecies has likely been extinct for almost 70 years. Many people have reported wild cougar sightings in the historical range of the eastern cougar; but evidence of these sightings suggests these animals are other subspecies, often of South American origin, and either escaped or were released from captivity, or are dispersing cougars from growing western populations. The Service (USFWS) will now prepare a proposal to remove eastern cougar from the endangered species list."

Bottom line: If they don't exist, they can't be endangered.

✦

Is there any possibility that cougars will ever again inhabit their old haunts in Maine? The prospect seems dim, especially in view of the drastically reduced deer situation. Without sufficient deer-wintering areas, which deer in these northern climes are dependent upon to get through Maine's tough winters, there will be scant prey base to support a breeding population. McCollough recently told me, "There are few working deer yards left in northern Maine." He claims a male cougar needs 44 deer each year to exist; females with cubs need 113. Plus, they require up to several hundred square miles of range.

McCollough offered one slight glimmer of hope for the future (given a recovery of the once-abundant deer herd). In a note to me: "The Florida panthers are doing very well and have reached carrying capacity of their habitat. More animals are dispersing northward, and one Florida panther was shot in Georgia last year. The Florida panther recovery plan calls for reestablishing two populations of 200-plus animals outside Florida in the Southeast. If that occurs, cats will easily travel up the Appalachians. Maybe they'll be as successful as coyotes at restoring historic range!"

Recently, Florida wildlife officials reported that 24 panthers had been killed in 2011, 9 due to collisions with vehicles. With a population of cougar numbering only about 150 to 160, to have 24 killed in one year is remarkable. (Which begs the question: If cougars are in Maine, why haven't any been found dead—along the highways or in the woods?)

Another recent development may throw all of this speculation into a loop. In the summer of 2011 a 140-pound cougar
was killed by a vehicle on the Wilbur Cross Parkway in Mil-
ford, Connecticut. (Connecticut residents have been reporting
a similar number of cougar sightings as Maine residents; this
was the first proof.) A necropsy (autopsy) disclosed this animal
had not been declawed and had other evidence this was a wild
animal, not a released captive.

Further study found that, amazingly, this was not an eastern, but a *western* cougar. Most astonishing? DNA evidence
proved a link to the population from the Black Hills of South
Dakota. DNA evidence from scat (droppings) and other data,
including hidden camera photos, also proved this cat had
traveled through Wisconsin and Minnesota on its long trek
east. According to McCollough, there was "an exact DNA
match with four genetic samples collected in Minnesota and
Wisconsin."

Imagine the dangers and obstacles this animal had to over-
come in its thousand-plus-mile journey: superhighways, major
rivers like the Mississippi and Hudson, etc., only to end its life
under the wheels of a vehicle on an eastern highway.

This individual animal, according to scientists, set a record
for dispersal (movement from its original territory).

In comparison, a move from Connecticut to Maine would be
just a relative hop, skip, and a jump for a roving-minded cougar.

What's my take on this? I *have* seen a live cougar in the wild.
Not in Maine, but in Wyoming, near Jackson Hole. It was an
incredible sight—climbing its way slowly up a hillside across
a stream, checking out every brush pile and clump of bushes
hunting for prey, its long switching tail and feline movements

very evident. It was a magnificent animal, well suited to its natural element.

The return of the cougar to Maine may not happen soon, but I remain optimistic.

A version of this story appeared in *Down East* magazine (August 2012).

3

How to Dupe an Enemy

Nature's Creatures as Masters of Deception

MODERN SCIENCE HAS DEVISED some remarkable techniques to aid the survival of humans in times of conflict, such as stealth aircraft and sophisticated camouflage. But we can only look with wonder and envy at the marvels nature provides both wild prey and predators for hiding from prying eyes.

What hikers of the wooded uplands haven't walked right by a still deer or rabbit without seeing it, nearly stepped on a snake or frog, or had the wits startled out of them by having the ground explode into the roaring takeoff of the ruffed grouse?

All hunters will tell you that the grouse's tactic works. Its thunderous departure leaves them gaping foolishly, shotguns hanging limply in their arms, as Br'er Partridge executes a dazzling aerial display, dodging behind trees and brush until it's out of sight—and shotgun range. The hunters are left to scratch their head in bafflement and wonder: How could they have missed seeing this rather large bird?

Besides employing fright psychology for eluding its enemies, the grouse is one of nature's masters of camouflage. Its dull-brown mottled plumage has the remarkable quality of becoming a part of the forest background. Whether crouched on the forest-floor leaf mold, flattened against the branch or trunk of a tree, or huddled like an extra bump on the mossy top of a rotting log, the grouse becomes invisible. Until it takes off. Then it psyches you out of a year's growth—and a partridge dinner. (In Maine, the ruffed grouse is commonly called the partridge.)

When such an encounter happened one day to my wife, Anita, it provided us with an apt demonstration of not only the animal world's great drive for self-survival, but also for perpetuation of the species.

It was a warmish May day in Maine. The two of us were walking near our home on a wooded hill, a place that had reverberated to the muffled drumming of courting grouse for several weeks. As Anita stepped past a clump of gray birches she was nearly knocked off her feet by thundering wings. A grouse had burst from the ground a foot away. When she regained her composure, she discovered the reason behind the bird's reluctance to depart until the last possible moment: This biddy had been brooding a clutch of newly laid eggs in a leaf-and-down-lined nest.

But our greatest surprise came a few days later when we cautiously approached the nest area. To our surprise, the nest had vanished. The leaves and forest detritus covered the ground in unbroken disorder, as if no nest had ever existed there.

Could it be that we had simply mistakenly identified the clump of trees? After all, gray birches have a rather nondescript sameness, and there were a lot of birches growing thereabouts. Though we circled and searched, we kept returning to one specific clump. We were certain the nest *had* been here. How could it have disappeared without a trace?

Fortunately, Anita was a persistent soul. She got down on hands and knees and studied the ground intently. Then she spotted a tiny clue: a small bit of down showing from under a leaf. With a twig she carefully parted the leaves to reveal the nest. The small eggs were carefully cushioned in down and feathers and covered over with leaves to keep them concealed and warm while mother was off to feed.

Some forms of natural protective coloration are obvious and well recognized: The polar bear, many mountain sheep and goats, and the snowy owl all wear permanent coats of white to blend with their almost perpetual environment of ice and snow.

When visiting northern Newfoundland one December, I found that the arctic version of grouse, the ptarmigan, had already assumed its white winter plumage, which replaces the brown feathers of summer. Thus protected, they appeared to have complete confidence in their safety. They permitted me to walk within a few feet of them while continuing to feed on berries under the snow.

Other common changelings to winter's protective white are the weasels (ermine, when white), snowshoe and arctic hares, and arctic foxes.

Less dramatic but equally effective is the change experienced each fall by the common white-tailed deer. Many is the experienced hunter who stalks—and fails to find—the red-haired deer he saw last summer. Nature's deception is at work again. It's easy to overlook the darker coats deer assume in fall and winter to better merge with the dark, somber northern forests of those seasons.

Color plays only a part in the effectiveness of camouflage. Mottling, striping, spots—these all aid in breaking up a creature's outlines and help it to dissolve into its background. The nesting grouse is a classic example; so is the defenseless dappled deer fawn. The spotted giraffe, striped zebra, and masked raccoon were not so clothed simply to dress up our zoos. Each is difficult for predators to see when the animal is on its home grounds.

Tough to spot, too, are the variegated snakes, lizards, and other reptiles that melt into backgrounds ranging from leaf-strewn forest ground to weed-infested marshes to decayed wood to sunbaked desert sand, rock, and ledge.

Perhaps the most bizarre forms of camouflage are found in the insect world. Some aquatic insects build tiny protective "homes" by gluing together bits of wood, stone, and other stream-bed debris. Here they live, hidden from the sharp eyes of foraging fish. Some spiders cover their burrow entrances with remarkable, concealing "trapdoors."

In addition to constructing nests of natural materials that blend in with the surroundings, birds have markings to fool their predators. The eggs of birds like terns, which nest in the open, are colored and speckled to merge with the nesting background—whether dried vegetation, sand, beach pebbles, or bare ledge. Gulls quickly remove newly hatched eggshells from the nest site, lest the white shell interiors attract sharp-eyed crows and other foraging predators to their tempting and vulnerable offspring.

Mimicry is a highly refined version of camouflage employed by some forms of wildlife. Among the most effective practitioners are certain moths and katydids, which, by remaining motionless, escape detection by resembling the branches, tree bark, or leaves to which they cling. The twig caterpillar holds itself stiffly angled from a limb, in startling imitation of a genuine branch twig.

Perhaps most deserving of a medal for mimicry, if only for its originality, is the small tropical frog which has developed a flattened shape and speckled, grayish coloration. Coupled with its propensity for lying motionless on a leaf throughout the daylight hours, this tiny night-foraging frog presents itself to the world as a remarkable likeness of the splash of a bird dropping.

Some creatures successfully use mimicry to dupe predators into believing they are inedible, or even dangerous. The harmless robber fly deceives hungry enemies with its close resemblance to the stinger-equipped bumblebee. Some inedible insects convey that information to predators by displaying vivid colors and distinctive markings. And certain mimetic flies, butterflies, and beetles escape capture by imitating the coloration and movements of other insects which have been found unpalatable by preying birds, animals, and other insects.

Two harmless but vivid southern snake species use bright coloration to fool predators and people into believing they are their venomous cousins. The scarlet king snake and the scarlet snake are often confused with the coral snake, which *is* venomous. All have red, black, and yellow bands. The difference is in the arrangements of the bands. People who work in the outdoors have developed mnemonic rhymes to help in identifying the harmless from the deadly: "Black head, you're dead." "If red touches yellow, it can kill a fellow." "If red touches black, it is a friend of Jack."

Various caterpillars and worms not only have brilliant eye-spots (often located near the tail), but they also bend or swell their bodies, rear up, and lash back and forth in mock savagery to frighten away would-be diners.

In a class by itself, however, is the world's most accomplished bluffer, the large sphinx moth. When threatened, it flashes open its wide-spreading wings to reveal two large, round markings—looking for all the world like the eyes of a large bird or animal. Apparently this strikes terror into the hearts of lesser predators, which usually prefer to take flight rather than attack so formidable an adversary. One of the obvious but still spectacular glamour guys in the world of natural camouflage is, of course, the chameleon. This master of changes can alter its coloration to match most backgrounds.

But there are other, lesser-known but equally fascinating quick-change artists to be found, particularly among the inhabitants of the underwater world. One of the more notable is the lowly flounder, which can produce spots, lines, and blotches to match its surrounding sea-floor home.

Tropical fishes reflect the brilliant hues of their coral reef environment. Shrimp, crabs, and lobsters take on the matching colors and mottling of bottom sands.

The pickerels and basses of freshwater ponds lurk in wait for unsuspecting prey from the obscurity of weeds and lily pads with which they merge into invisibility. Even the vivid-hued trout of clear streams vary in the degree of coloration of the vermiculated markings of the back scales, the better to blend in with the light or dark stream bottoms. And why the whitish bellies of some fish? To lessen visibility from underneath, against the brightness of sky and light water surface.

Occasionally, nature goofs. Mutants are born which deviate from the inherent family characteristics of color or shape. Sometimes, as in forms of crustacea, imbalances of body chemistry result in strangely hued individuals. In addition to facing hostility from their own kind, such misfits are in constant danger of swift detection and annihilation by predators.

While these phenomena are fascinating and sometimes exotic, there are lessons in natural survival to be learned from the familiar creatures found close to home.

As I lazily enjoyed a spring day, I was startled to see one of the dandelion flowers in my sadly neglected lawn suddenly take flight in the form of a bobolink. Later I observed the bird feeding on the flowers, the yellow patch at the back of its head looking for all the world like just another flower nodding in the breeze. Its body, thanks to my negligent caretaking with the mower, was well concealed by the longish grass. Thus it fed, in comparative safety from detection.

Survival often means that wildlife must employ supplementary diversion along with camouflage to deceive hungry predators. Such was demonstrated when a pair of killdeer moved into the pasture a few hundred feet from my house.

Whenever one of the neighbor's cats, dogs, or cattle came along, the killdeer went into a frenzy of excitement, running about their feet, flying at their heads, and circling the pasture in swift, erratic flight—all the while piercing the air with their characteristic, loud *killdee-ee-ee*. By watching them for several days with binoculars, we finally located their nest and crept down to look at the tiny, speckled eggs. They resembled pebbles in the grass.

In time, the killdeers' distraction behavior intensified. Now they landed a few feet from the intruder and fell upon their sides, fluttering and holding up a "crippled" wing to reveal its light underside to lure the intruder from the nest area.

When we spotted the young chicks, they were miniature replicas of their parents. Once we approached, they froze and remained locked in immobility. And, thanks to their barred breasts and dull plumage, they blended so well with the pasture grasses as to be impossible to spot from distances of more than a few feet.

Science tells us that these many wondrous forms and varieties of protective markings and behavior are the result of millions of years of evolutionary adaptation and natural selection. In the wild creatures' world, the most visible prey are swiftly eliminated. The better-adapted and camouflaged are left to propagate and strengthen the species' strains of protective color, markings, and behavior. It might be said that discretion is truly the better part of survival.

4

Our Neighbors Were Bandits

Petty Larceny on the Shores of Brassua Lake

WILD BANDITS SURROUNDED our modest little cabin home in northern Maine. Some of them even wore masks. These larcenous neighbors were the birds and the animals surrounding our sporting camps on the shores of Brassua Lake, in the remote Moosehead Lake region. But from the very day that we moved in, back in the spring of 1955, we welcomed the wild freeloaders at a big, sturdy bird-feeding station just outside our living-room window.

Naturally, the winter birds led our flock of neighborhood greeters. The tough little chickadees came first, robbing each other right and left, until they were driven away by the larger juncos. Close behind them were the bigger and bolder holdup artists, claiming priority in the chow line by virtue of size and pugnacity. These were the blue jays and Canada jays, also known as gorbies, moosebirds, whiskey-jacks, and camp robbers.

The latter name is a well-deserved one. Canada jays love to hang around camping grounds, and I've known them to swoop down and steal food right out of my plate or frying pan.

Birds of a Feather

Unwrapping a sandwich in the most desolate part of the woods is a signal for one or more Canada jays to appear magically out of nowhere, intent upon snatching the human food.

Canada jays will follow a hunter for miles through the woods, flitting silently from tree to tree, sometimes behind, sometimes ahead, but always keeping the hunter in sight. This nerve-wracking habit led old-time Maine lumberjacks to look upon the gorbies with awe, believing them to be the reincarnation of dead comrades. Hence, killing a gorbie was sure to bring ill luck to the perpetrator of the foul deed. A few backwoodsmen still insist that the hunter who kills a gorbie will never again bag a deer.

Despite his rascally reputation, however, the jay performs a useful service, as do most forms of wildlife. He is a scavenger, helping in his small way to keep our forests clean. During the deer-hunting season, I have frequently observed jays at the scene of recent kills, making frenzied efforts to haul away the offal left by the hunters after they'd field-dressed their game.

As the snowdrifts disappeared that first spring, the migratory birds found their way to our clearing and the feeding station: robins and bluebirds, various species of sparrows and swallows, the finches, flickers, and warblers. Soon our little corner of the woods was ringing with their cacophony of loud, rich, and sweet notes, with overtones of raucous cawing from the crows and hoarse croaking from their larger, more ragged, but equally sooty first cousins, the ravens. These black bandits were much too wary to come to the feeder, but they hung around the edge of the clearing or along the shore, watching for their turn at pillaging.

Right away my wife Anita took over the management of our bird-feeding station and put into it everything that appeared even remotely edible. Stale bread crumbs, biscuits, doughnuts, cake, pieces of pie, leftovers ranging from spaghetti to clam chowder, and various culinary accidents all found hungry takers. The jays were even crazy about dog food.

Meanwhile, our pseudo cocker spaniel Rusty appointed herself protector of the property and spent hours in fruitless bird chases before she realized that they operated in a separate dimension. Conceding defeat, she settled into peaceful coexistence with the bird population.

Although her war against squirrels was equally abortive, she never relented in this campaign. Directly under the living-room window where the feeder was located, I neglected to replace a removable panel where the water pipes enter the house. Rusty took over that space in which to lie in ambush. The scampering feet of a squirrel never failed to bring Rusty out of that hole, but the squirrels always hopped into a tree ahead of her eager jaws and jeered from its topmost branches, while the dog ran around in circles, yipping in frustration

Squirrels, of course, are more notorious and persistent thieves than the jays. But as time passed, the squirrels took second place. No other species of wildlife provided our household—including Rusty—with as much excitement as the raccoons.

These notorious panhandlers were constant visitors from the time they came out of hibernation until cold weather drove them back to deep sleep in the fall. We had unlimited opportunity to study them and had ringside seats at innumerable coon fights. There is no honor among these masked thieves. I've watched female raccoons knock their youngsters off the feeder, the better to stuff their own mouths with both paws. Hitting the ground with an audible thump, the youngsters would bounce back on their feet, charge up to the feeder, and light into the old lady with a ferocity equal to hers. The snarls and growls that accompanied these family battles were terrifying.

Raccoons display an uncanny intellect and an amazing dexterity with their front paws. They are also intensely curious and mischievous, as they often proved through their tireless forays into our garbage cans. We could not count the nights when we were awakened by the sound of a garbage can being knocked over. Crawling out of bed to investigate in the certainty that, this time, it must be a bear, we've invariably found that the marauders were our friends, the coons.

Anita tried jamming the covers onto the rubbish cans so hard that she couldn't take them off herself, but the coons were never stumped. Almost every morning we'd find the can knocked over, the cover off, and refuse littered all over the yard.

Another trick the raccoons mastered was to rob the fishermen of their live bait, usually kept in two sectional pails, one inside the other. When fishermen planned to keep minnows overnight, they tied a connecting rope to the handles of both sections, put a heavy rock in the outside pail to weight it down on the edge of the dock, then dropped the inner, minnow-filled bucket into the lake. But the raccoons often pulled the liner up by the rope, released the catch on the cover, and enjoyed a live fish dinner. They were extremely fond of angleworms, and when one summer's guest left his bait box outside one night, he found the coons had not only eaten his worms but also devoured the commercial compound in which they were being kept alive.

Raccoons are such gluttons that they will eat practically anything that flies, walks, swims, crawls, or lies dead. I've watched dozens of coons eating. They sit on top of a trash can, stuffing garbage down their throats as fast as they can swallow.

⸙

We became convinced that the widespread belief that raccoons always wash their food is sheer myth. There was a large lake directly in front of our house and a brook a few yards from the bird-feeding station, but we never saw a coon leave the feeder to wash his food.

True, I have seen raccoons dunk their food into water that was right at hand, but I doubt that it was for any hygienic reason. A local woodsman, whose observations I respect, believes that since taste is associated with smell, and wetting food releases more of its odor, the coons derive double pleasure from food dunked before eating. His theory may be all wet, but I'll accept it until a more plausible one is offered.

The mischievous stunts of our raccoons were endless. They opened unlatched doors easily, simply hooking the door frame with their claws and pulling it open. One of their favorite pastimes was to climb on the porches of the guest cabins and pose for flash pictures, in return for which they would steal any food they could get.

Another endearing little habit of theirs was to drop from a tree onto the roof of a cabin in the middle of the night, then scamper around playfully. Since some big coons weigh in the neighborhood of forty pounds, this trick was not particularly entertaining to insomniacs.

One summer, a middle-aged artist and his wife from New York occupied one of our tent sites. They arrived late in the day, and I neglected to warn them about the raccoons. Before retiring that night, the campers piled all of their food on a picnic table and, of course, they discovered next morning that they'd been robbed of everything edible, including a whole chicken.

However, they were delighted when they learned the identity of the robbers, and hurried down to Rockwood to replenish their supplies—including a large stock of food for the masked bandits. That night they loaded the table with a coon banquet, kept the campfire going, and stayed awake far into the night to watch. They reported that six coons sat on the table feasting at one time, while the shining eyes of several others peered down from the trees.

That couple probably needed a second vacation to rest up after their two weeks with us, for they stayed up until the small hours every night, watching the raccoons in fascination. Each day they pursued a full schedule of fishing, boating, sketching, hunting driftwood, hiking, and bird- and animal-watching. But they were lured mostly by the nocturnal revels of the coons.

A male coon, whom we called Sam, was our most frequent visitor. He was so brazen that he even visited our feeding station in broad daylight, contrary to the raccoon nature. When Sam had devoured all of the food on the feeder, he had the habit of knocking on our window to ask for more. If we failed to respond, he waddled back a couple of feet, plopped down onto his chubby bottom, and stared intently through the window until one of us passed by, whereby he'd scramble up and resume rapping to get our attention.

Sam was entirely aware, of course, of the threat to his well-being imposed by Rusty. He always surveyed the scene carefully to make sure that the dog was safely inside the house before strolling boldly up to the feeder in the daytime to dine at his leisure.

⊸⧓⊷

Rusty, who hated all coons collectively, had an obsessive personal feud with Sam. The little dog regularly climbed onto a table to watch the coons through the window when they were on the feeder. Occasionally, when she couldn't contain herself any longer, she'd charge full tilt into the window, snarling and barking, which usually made the more-nervous coons leave the feeder temporarily. But not Sam, who knew that the window-pane was a safe barrier.

Once, an unusually loud commotion brought us to the living room to witness Rusty's humiliation. We found her, cheek pressed against the windowpane, fangs bared wickedly, emitting the wild, bloodcurdling sounds that raccoons never fail to entice from her. On the opposite side, Sam's shiny black nose was pressed against the glass, and he was staring her out of countenance. As we watched, he slowly and sardonically turned away, casually brushed his tail across the window in front of Rusty several times, and contentedly waddled off about his business. The dog had hysterics.

Since raccoons are vicious fighters, and often maim or kill well-trained hunting dogs, we always took precautions to prevent our small dog from meeting one head-on. But inevitably it happened, on the days we failed to survey the coon situation before letting her out. The first time it occurred, Rusty was on sentry duty in her hole under the house when we were jerked from our chairs by an unearthly, high-pitched shriek, which we identified as Rusty's "coon yodel." It was a paralyzing sound, embodying terror, hatred, and murderous intent, such as I've never heard from any other animal.

By the time I had recovered sufficiently to rush outside, Rusty was throwing herself madly against the sides of the feeder, still shrieking demonically. A monstrous old male coon slowly moved to the edge of the feeder, gripped its edge with his toenails, leaned way out, and insultingly nipped her on the nose! At the same instant, the coon launched himself into a tremendous leap that carried him fully fifteen feet away. But the instant he touched the ground, Rusty was on top of him, still screaming, and they went rolling end over end in a wild tangle of legs and gleaming, lashing fangs.

I raced after them, arming myself at the woodpile en route. By the time I caught up with them, the coon was frantically scooting up a tree, where he hung from a limb in absolute terror. Rusty threw herself in impotent rage against the bole of the tree, tearing at its bark and sustaining her murderous shrieks until, after repeated efforts, I succeeded in calming her and dragging her away.

To our relief and amazement, she hadn't a scratch on her—not even a mark where she'd been nipped on the nose. Her miraculous escape from this, and far too many similar fracases with raccoons, must have been due to her amazing speed. Once roused, Rusty was the fastest-moving animal on four legs that it has ever been my privilege to watch in action.

She dauntlessly persisted in her role as watchdog, despite the fact that our thieving neighbors were legion, and ranged from tiny field mice, fully as great a nuisance as their city-bred cousins, to an occasional wandering bear. One of our more unusual visitors was a young fox that developed the habit of coming to our back door every evening one fall, shyly seeking a handout.

Other particularly interesting highwaymen in our domain was the mink family that resided near the dam on Moose River. The entire tribe had feasted on many a trout or salmon that some fisherman had carelessly left lying on the bank while he resumed his angling. One fall my brother had to keep a particularly brazen mink at bay with a fishing rod after the little monster had stolen one of his trout, cached it under a nearby brush pile, and returned to make repeated efforts to steal the rest of his catch.

There was no letup in the raids that took place in our neck of the woods. Some of our robber neighbors went winging south in the wintertime, others into hibernation. But there were many furred and feathered crooks that kept pillaging, day and night, summer and winter, keeping the three of us on our toes—and paws.

An earlier version of this story appeared in
Down East magazine (March 1964).

5

Tracks in the Snow

When What You See Is Only Half the Story

WINTER. ICE JAMS up the waterways, and snow lies deep on
Maine woodlands. This is the time to study tracks in the snow
and perhaps find the elusive "snow snake." To the experienced
and observant eye, these signs tell the stories of the lives of
animals that remain awake, active, and hopefully alive during
the coldest season.

It requires a bit of effort to read these hidden chapters of the
winter wilderness drama. The best "vehicle" to enable us to "get
there from here" is that marvelous device developed by Native
Americans, the snowshoe. Especially useful is the somewhat
oblong, tail-less style called the bearpaw.

I've spent much time on cross-country skis and snowmobiles
to navigate over the snow, but the bearpaw's great advantage
is its ability to bring you deep into the dense tangles of brush
and thick growth where snow machines can't go and long skis
are too easily snagged. Bearpaws are the first choice of timber
cruisers who need to make quick turns and buck through the
thick stuff.

Snowshoes make it possible to float over blowdowns and tangles of brush that, buried under feet of snow, would be virtually impenetrable on foot in the warm seasons. These clusters are also the favored haunts of many creatures that seek their protection from prying—and preying—eyes.

A pair of snowshoes got me to wintering bear dens, in the company of a biological research crew. We visited one such den in northern Maine buried under more than four feet of snow. The crew located the site by listening for the signals from the female's radio collar. They dug out the den, tranquilized the mom, and briefly removed her and her two cubs. They then took and recorded the bears' vital statistics before returning them to their snug home, reburying them under the thick, protective layer of snow to await the arrival of spring.

You don't have to move far from traveled roads to find wildlife tracks in the snow. Among the most frequent, naturally, will be the hopping tracks of squirrels and rabbits. But to find deer tracks, if the snow is deep, you'll have to head to areas of heavy coniferous forests, whose thick canopy prevents much of the snow from reaching the ground. Here, in the protection of the evergreens, the deer tread down paths to reach their favorite food, cedar. When snow gets much over eighteen inches deep, the animals' bellies scrape the snow as they walk and they are thus forced to retreat to these deer yards. Big, long-legged moose prefer to winter on higher ground. Their yards are often found on the sides of ridges. One of the biggest I ever found, near Moosehead Lake, was located in a hemlock grove on the southern slope of a hill. This afforded the moose protection from cold northerly winds and a chance to soak up heat from the sun on warmer days.

A mystery to beginning trackers is the little, thrusted-up ridge of snow winding through the woods and across fields. Brush the snow away and you'll find a tiny snow tunnel, probably created by a foraging woods mouse traveling from burrow to burrow, or leading to a source of seeds. In this way mice are protected from cold and wind as well as hungry and sharp-eyed foxes, wildcats, hawks, and owls. But not always. Some predators are equipped with such keen hearing that they can detect the skittering sounds of rodents moving under the snow, allowing them to plunge down through several inches and nab their prey with pinpoint accuracy.

Sometimes, early snows are too thin to tunnel under and actually more easily reveal the dark-furred mice to predators. Then the tiny footprints end abruptly, with wing-feather marks on the snow showing where an owl has located its meal on a frozen January night. Such encounters are swift, silent, and merciful.

There are innumerable other tracks and signs in winter's woods, some easily identifiable and others puzzling. On a warmish day you might find the tracks of a raccoon, an animal that normally spends much of the winter asleep; however, it's not a true hibernator, and will occasionally take a midwinter stroll.

Following a bad storm, you might find a sizable hole in a snowbank. Around it are clumps of snow, signs of an explosion of sorts. This is where a ruffed grouse (known as "partridge" to Mainers) rode out the storm. It plopped into the bank and allowed snow to drift in over it to seal out the cold. The bird slept warm and cozy in its own down "sleeping bag."

Sometimes a glance is enough for the experienced woodsman to identify the animal that passed. A fox plants its feet precisely so that each print lands along a straight line. Tracks of wildcats and other felines such as lynx seldom show claw marks, while those of dogs and coyotes show them prominently.

Minks, weasels, fishers, and marten leave wide-spaced hopping tracks. And those "snow snake" tracks are made by their cousin, the otter, which travels by sliding over the snow and leaving furrows to confuse us. The ever-playful otter sometimes utilizes a steep bank to create a "slide" which it repeatedly climbs and slides down to its apparent great delight. Not all animal life is sheer survival.

But the otter, the beaver, and the muskrat prefer to spend most of the winter swimming under the ice, coming up to air holes and pockets to breathe. The reason? Their oily fur coats are perfectly waterproof. And that water temperature is actually much warmer than the air, which can dip to 20 or 30 below zero.

Previously published in the *Christian Science Monitor*. (1969)

6

Superior Scents

The Mysterious Gift of Smell in the Animal Kingdom

IT WAS ON THE COLDEST, wildest night of a bad winter that my wife and I got a brief and momentarily hair-raising glimpse into one of the mysterious ways in which nature's creatures use their sense of smell to ensure their existence. Our cabin, on the shore of a remote northern Maine lake, was being buffeted by a northwest wind of near gale force that swept down the nine mile expanse of lake ice. The thermometer outside the cabin registered a numbing 20 degrees below zero.

To make things worse, the frigid blast was chewing into a foot of snow that had been dumped over the area earlier in the day, filling the air with light, fluffy, blinding flakes. No sane person would be abroad on such a night, so the last thing we expected was a visitor. Anita and I were spending a quiet evening in the living room, reading, when we were jerked upright in our seats by a long-drawn-out, quavering howl just outside the back door. Our cocker spaniel, Rusty, came charging out from behind the stove where she'd been snoozing, and stood with her hair bristling and a menacing growl rumbling deep in her throat.

Startled, I grabbed a flashlight, went quickly to the window, and scraped a peephole in the frost. Aiming the beam outside, I peered into the churning, snow-laden air but could see nothing. Meanwhile, Anita had opened the kitchen door a crack and poked her flashlight outside. I heard her exclaim, "Why, it's Terrio's dog!"

Incredulous, I took a look. Sure enough, there was a dog sitting by the woodshed, and I recognized him as belonging to a family that lived a few miles away in the village of Rockwood. We slammed the door shut and stood looking down at Rusty. The mystery was solved.

Rusty, a female, was still a pup when we'd acquired her, and we'd never had her spayed. She was in heat. Terrio's dog had come a-courting! He camped in our woodshed for the better part of a week—one of the coldest weeks in the memory of the oldest residents in this notoriously cold region of northwestern Maine.

The amazing thing is that although the dog had never been to our cabin before, he had become aware of Rusty's condition without any loss of time, and had made his way to our place on the most violent night of a violent winter. And he did that by literally following his nose through several miles of unfamiliar wilderness.

⬥

The highly acute sense of smell of most animals and insects is a constant wonder to scientist and layman alike. The lowliest cur slinking down an alley lives in a world of scent of which we are completely ignorant; it possesses a gift that has been denied we "superior" humans.

The fox trotting down a woodland path is reading and interpreting the story of life that goes on around him more clearly than we are able to read the words of books. His nose tells him what creatures have traveled the path ahead, how long ago they passed, what they were doing, and even some of their personal characteristics—their sex, age, and probably even a fair indication of their physical condition. Tiny threads of pungent odor drifting in from the surrounding woodlands keep him apprised of the goings-on of a wide area around him. His ultrasensitive nostrils inform him of the proximity of enemies or the presence of potential meals, and in season lead him unerringly to a mate.

Scent plays a major role in the sex life of many creatures.

Male canines, such as the dog that visited us, are lured to receptive females from astonishing distances by an irresistible scent released in the female's urine.

Many animals depend on their scent as both a lure and a sex stimulus. Female deer attract bucks by emitting a potent musk. The desire of elephants is heightened by the discharge of a substance from a gland located on the bull's head. Weasels, minks, muskrats, otters, fishers, and wolverines are stimulated by musk. And the beaver's castoreum is used by trappers to lure all manner of animals to their sets. Even that notoriously scented woods kitty, the skunk, employs musk in its lovemaking.

If you think Rusty's would-be boyfriend performed quite a feat when he found his way to our cabin that wild night, the olfactory powers of some members of the insect world would seem to verge on the fantastic. There is a species of moth, for instance, that can catch the scent of a female ten miles away and make a beeline flight to her. Furthermore, the males won't bother to show up unless she's an unmated virgin!

Some animals use scent as a sort of crude communication system.

All members of the canine clan keep track of each other with "scent posts"—low bushes, stumps, and posts along their trails. No canine will pass one without stopping to sniff the information left there by previous wanderers, and won't leave before depositing its own sign. The city dog's hydrants and lampposts serve the same purpose.

Shrewd trappers take advantage of this trait by concealing a trap at the base of a post and sprinkling the post with a scent concocted from animal glands. Trappers prefer to use the glands of animals from another area; they say that the scent of a stranger is a surefire attractor.

Many of the musk-carrying animals have similar methods of communication. Muskrats deposit their powerful, sweetish musk on logs and mud banks. Beavers build a mound of mud at the water's edge on which to place their castoreum. Otters keep tabs on each other by depositing a few drops of musk from their anal glands on tufts of grass.

And wolverines, notoriously solitary and pugnacious creatures, stake out their hunting territory by marking the boundaries with musk. These serve as a "keep out" warning to other predators searching for new hunting territories. Most interlopers heed the warning.

Scent also serves some animals as a defensive weapon—the skunk, for example. From a pair of anal glands it emits a fine spray of a most offensive fluid, and is able to aim in any direction by contorting its body. Its aim is deadly up to fifteen feet.

Skunks are not the only animals that discharge scent under stress. Alarmed or angry snakes release it from glands under the base of the tail. Excited weasels and minks project a nauseating scent. And so does their cousin of the far north, the wolverine. It merely has to appear on the scene to drive off bears, cougars, and bands of wolves from their fresh kills. After gorging itself on the meat, the wolverine fouls it with its own repulsive scent, to make sure that no other animal will feed on it.

Scent plays a vital role for most creatures in the search for food and the detection of enemies. We only need watch a hound trailing a rabbit or a bird dog casing up on a covey of quail to realize that their actions are merely refinements of the methods used by their forebears to find sustenance. Deer and bears, which have relatively poor eyesight, can smell hunters over astonishing distances.

But here again, the insects excel. Many, including bees and cockroaches, have a sensitive smelling apparatus inside small knobs on the ends of their antennae, which they weave around to sample the shifting air currents for airborne food trails. The bee even has smelling/tasting nerves in its feet. Those two senses are so closely intermingled, even in humans, as to practically merge into one. Moreover, if a worker bee stumbles onto an exceptionally rich food source, it opens a tiny, gland-lined pocket in its abdomen and excretes a scent on which other bees can accurately home in.

Even fish have an efficient sense of smell. Scientists trying to find out how fish are able to locate food in roily water have discovered that many species can actually discern odors at various points on their bodies—some with their tails. This might explain why fish are frequently foul-hooked in their sides or bellies. The angler probably jerked the hook just as the fish snuggled up to the bait for an exploratory sniff.

An elderly woodsman neighbor, a keen observer who has spent a lifetime studying wildlife, told me his pet theory regarding the motivation behind a peculiar habit of one of our more common wild animals, the raccoon. Practically everyone has seen raccoons washing their food before eating. I've watched them while they held a piece of food underwater for minutes at a time, rolling it over and over and fondling it gently with their paws before finally consuming it.

Coons are not, however, so fastidious when they find something edible away from water. They frequently prowl around trash dumps miles away from water and feed on half-putrid garbage. The theory of our woodsman friend is that the coons dunk their food when water is handy to make it more tasty, since wetting food releases more of its odor.

Humans weren't the only creatures shortchanged in the nose department. Many birds appear to have a relatively undeveloped sense of smell, depending almost entirely on their keen eyesight for locating food and spotting predators. Hawks and owls frequently prey on skunks and appear to relish them. Naturalists have debated for years on the question of whether vultures find carrion by scent.

Cornell University ornithologists used to think that vultures had very poor smelling ability and found their high-smelling provisions by sight, even when the carcass was almost completely hidden under dense brush. They now say the birds fly low to sense the odor of carrion.

The feline family also appears to have poorly developed smelling apparatus. Trappers say wildcats and lynx often walk right by baited trap-sets with no apparent hesitation in their stride. The trappers take advantage of the cats' keen eyes and innate curiosity by hanging a rabbit skin or feather above the set. This is called an attractant. Then it is more likely to investigate the lure, to its regret.

In times of famine, however, the cats have been known to dig up and feed on carcasses buried under the snow, which would be difficult to find unless they were smelled. This brings up the possibility that the cats, which evidently like their meat hot and fresh, simply aren't interested in the frozen bait unless driven by hunger.

Most dog owners who live in the country are only too well aware that a dog can seldom bypass any carrion it finds in the woods without stopping to roll and rub itself in it, smearing its fur with the foul putrefaction. Here the dog is blindly following an instinct handed down from its wild ancestors. It is attempting to disguise its own odor so that it won't betray itself to its prey—a fairly common habit among many predators. The felines accomplish the same end in a more socially acceptable manner: They wash themselves frequently, keeping their telltale body odor down to a minimum.

Strangely, the smeared dog's fetid aura doesn't seem to blunt its own powers of smell to any marked degree. Befouled dogs appear able to hunt and to identify elusive odors with an apparently unimpaired sensitivity.

Indeed, this highly developed ability to isolate and identify odors is what we less richly endowed humans find most amazing and difficult to comprehend about animals. Any dog can easily pick its master out of a crowd by scent alone.

Bloodhounds, after being given a sniff of an individual's article of clothing, have unerringly followed that person's faint thread of scent along crowded streets without becoming confused. Evidently each of us has our own personal odor, which can identify us to animals as clearly as do our fingerprints or DNA.

Through experimentation and observation, I found that even our little dog, Rusty—descendant of a breed not as noted for its trailing ability as, say, the hounds—possessed this ability to an astonishing degree. We operated a summer camp and campground at our place, and during the summer there were usually a lot of people around. Frequently, when Anita was busy at some remote cabin or campsite, I'd let Rusty out of the house several hours after she'd left and then watch as the dog followed Anita's wandering footsteps, crisscrossed by our guests' scent trails, without any apparent difficulty. Rusty never failed to track her down.

Rusty was not exceptional. Originally, she was the runt of a very nondescript litter, and spent the first few weeks of her life in the cellar of an elderly bachelor's farmhouse, nearly starved and lorded over by her larger littermates. The first few days in our home were a nightmare, which she spent cowering under a bed.

But she was a completely transformed dog when we started taking her outside. Here was a fascinating new world of sights—and especially scents. Every bush, twig, leaf, and blade of grass had to be investigated and sniffed. Here she could trace trails where field mice, moles, and squirrels had scurried through the leaves. She would push her nose into a pile of dead leaves and drink in the various scents much as a *bon vivant* savors the bouquet of an exquisite liquor.

On our frequent rambles through the nearby woods she was constantly ranging the trail ahead and the woods on each side. And her wide-flaring, all-knowing nostrils were never at rest, continually vacuuming up great drafts of the richly scented forest air and analyzing its infinite subtle odors, sifting and interpreting and reliving the complex stories of life with a clarity unknown to us. Her marvelous nose told her, though there was no visible sign of it, that a family of field mice had set up housekeeping deep inside that dead tree; that here, under this clump of bushes, was a favorite run of the local snowshoe hares; and there, on the tiny sandy spot where the warm sun splashes down between the treetops, was the favored sunning spot of a certain grouse. Meanwhile, we stumbled by blindly, unknowing.

I think the distinction between Rusty's mysterious world and ours manifested itself most clearly when we went out on the lake for an evening canoe ride. As we glided silently over the glass-calm water along the shore, even our blunted olfactory nerves were constantly assailed by an ever-changing scent picture of the forest, borne to us on the perpetual, barely perceptible drift of air coming down from the ridge. We would detect a whiff of wood smoke from the cabin chimney, the rich aroma of forest earth and decaying vegetation, or a mere hint of spruce.

At such times Rusty stood in the canoe with her forepaws on the shoreward gunwale, nostrils working audibly as she "read" the air. By watching her closely—and exercising a little imagination—we got a hint of the story of life that was being enacted up on the ridge. Her tail would come up and start wagging happily. Perhaps she recognized a squirrel or a fox, both of which she delighted in chasing and never catching.

Farther along the shore she would stiffen, nose probing high in the air, and whine. Could this have been the scent of a grouse, arousing the faint bird-dog instinct retained from some obscure ancestor? Still farther on she'd again stiffen, but this time her hackles would rise and she'd growl threateningly. Perhaps a raccoon, sneaking up to raid our bird feeder, or a bear feeding on the ridge. She abhorred both of these animals with a slow-burning and consuming hatred.

It was at such times, seeing Rusty so alive and so all-aware, that we stood at the very brink of the animal world and sampled the mysterious gift of animal scent.

A version of this story first appeared in *Field & Stream* (July 1961).

7

Lombard's Log Hauler

A Mainer Invents the World's First Snowmobile

I'VE BEEN TOLD that the snowmobile was invented in Minnesota during the 1940s. Some people claim that it first came into existence in Canada in the 1920s.

I say that's all wrong. The first powered snow-traveling vehicle was in use over a hundred years ago, and this fantastic vehicle—designed to help revolutionize warfare and make it literally possible for men to "move the earth"—was the brainchild of a brilliant native of the State of Maine.

True, Alvin Lombard's monstrous steam log haulers bore scant resemblance to today's sleek and sassy snow bugs; nevertheless, they possessed the basic ingredients of a successful machine: an engine for propulsion, a mechanism for steering, and tracks capable of moving the vehicle over snow-covered ground.

They were not known for speed or beauty, but the Lombards made up for their charming ugliness with prodigious strength. Old-time woodsmen who saw them at work in the snowy northern forests related amazing tales of long trains of log sleds winding their way through frozen days and crackling nights, to the accompaniment of chuffing steam power.

The Lombard was apparently the world's first successful application of the lag tread, which since has provided the world with its military tanks, tractors, bulldozers, and power shovels reshaping the face of this scarred, old Earth. The modern snowmobile tread is itself a modification of the lag track.

Before Lombard came along to revolutionize it, winter woods travel had shown scant progress in centuries. Men had the choice of crude cross-country skis developed in the Scandinavian countries, the snowshoes of the American Indians, or the Eskimos' dog teams. Wood hauling was done by laboriously slow teams of oxen or horses, which were forced to toil under brutally harsh conditions. Few survived more than a season or two in the woods.

Alvin Orlando Lombard was born in 1856 on a small farm in Springfield, deep in the woods of eastern Maine. His upbringing apparently was typical of backcountry farm boys of that period. Alvin's father was a sawmill operator as well as a blacksmith. Apparently by watching and assisting him, the keen-witted son gained an early sensitivity to the feel and mechanics of wood and metal.

Not much is known about Lombard's early years, but there are published reports that while still a young teenager, he did a man's job in his father's mill. He is said to have built a miniature sawmill on a small brook on the family farm. It was fully operational, and used to slice "boards" from cucumbers grown in the family garden. By the time Lombard reached his forties, in the late 1890s, then residing in the papermaking town of Waterville, Maine, he was a successful inventor holding a number of important patents. Most of his inventions were in the form of wood-handling and production machinery. One of his most important contributions to technology was a complex device still in use for controlling hydroelectric turbines.

It wasn't until 1899 that Lombard began working on his log-hauling monster. Steam, at that time the giant of industrial power, was his logical choice. In fact, Alvin Lombard is credited with having built a steam auto before those other two Maine inventors, the Stanley brothers.

By this time, steam locomotives had tamed the West, crossed the Great Divide, and formed lifelines connecting the remotest corners of the country. But locomotives were restricted to operating on carefully engineered and constructed rail beds, with slight grades. They were far too costly and impractical for woods operations.

Lombard's prototype, which he named the "Mary Anne," made its woods debut during the winter hauling season of 1900–01. It could haul, but it had one major flaw: The horse still hadn't been entirely eliminated. A team of horses had to be hitched ahead of the engine to steer the front runners, due to the engine's great weight.

He finally eliminated the horses by installing a geared-down steering mechanism handled by a rugged lumberjack who sat out in the open on a wooden box set above the front runners.

This steersman was the unsung hero of the steam Lombard era. The only concession to his comfort in later models was an open-fronted wooden cab built around his seat box. The front remained open because it was his only means of escape if his heavy, unwieldy vehicle ran away with a heavy load on a downgrade.

For the first two decades of the twentieth century, Lombards moved forests of wood to supply Maine's paper and lumber mills. The steamers hauled long trains of log-laden sleds on hauling roads kept iced down by watering crews which patrolled with water-tank sleds at night. "Trains" of a dozen or more sleds, carrying 300 tons or more of wood, were not uncommon. Turnouts, similar to railroad sidings, were provided for tractors hauling back empty sleds to allow the passage of loaded trains. On some permanent hauling roads, dual lanes were built—the predecessors of today's divided-lane highways.

Big woods operations used the more-efficient coal to fire their Lombard steamers, but many small jobs stuck to cheaper wood. By the 1920s, steam was losing ground to the internal combustion engine, so Lombard began building gasoline-powered tractors. His tractors were now used for plowing snow and hauling earth.

Alvin Orlando Lombard may have been the first to develop and patent a tracked crawler-type vehicle, but his patent proved less ironclad than did the boilers on his steam haulers. Soon, other companies across the country had copied his idea, and the era of the bulldozer was born.

Lombard's Traction and Engine Company factory was located on the site of the former Keyes Fibre Company in Waterville. Several years ago I saw what may be one of the last relics of the Lombard era at Waterville: a Lombard snowplow once used for street-clearing by the municipal government.

Most of Lombard's log haulers have long since met their demise under the sputter of junkmen's cutting torches. A few are said to be rotting and rusting away in remote corners of the Maine woods.

One of the best-preserved steam haulers was stored for many years at Clayton Lake in northern Maine. It is now on public display at the Lumbermen's Museum at Ashland. Another steam Lombard may be seen at the woods museum in

Patten—this one made up from parts of several machines found at long-abandoned logging camps of that region and hauled to the museum for assembly.

With its acquisition of the Allagash Wilderness Waterway, the State of Maine took over ownership of several gasoline Lombard tractors stored in a shed at Churchill Lake Dam.

And those are about all that remains as testimony to this genius of Maine, a man whose inventions freed the horse from centuries of killing toil and gave humans the means of literally changing the face of the world. And, of course, gave the world its first snowmobile.

Author's note: *More than a century after the last Lombard steam log hauler was silenced in the northern Maine woods, the huff and chuff of a steam Lombard can still be seen and heard. The late contractor, Harry C. Crooker of Brunswick, spent several years in the 1960s and '70s searching the North Woods, usually by snowmobile, for artifacts and relics of the old lumbering era. One was a near-junk Lombard he acquired and restored to original running condition. For years, that Lombard tractor has been displayed and operated at Maine fairs and lumbering events to allow the public to get a glimpse of the ungainly machine. His sons and their friends usually operate it.*

8

Nature's Mysterious Misfits

Accounting for the Strange Behaviors of Wildlife

ONE SEPTEMBER NIGHT, a tremendous bull moose was jogging along the highway some three miles from our cabin in northern Maine when he saw a big logging truck bearing down on him. Without a moment's hesitation the bull lowered his massive antlers and charged straight into the glaring headlights. Result: one dead moose, and one heavily damaged truck.

A neighbor of ours was busy in her kitchen one day that same fall when she heard a loud crash in the living room. She was startled, but being a woman of fortitude, she investigated. In the living room she found the wind whistling through a jagged hole in the window and the carpet covered with glass. Among the shards was a large, very dead, partridge.

There's nothing unique about these two incidents. I chose them at random because they occurred close by, when we were living in northern Maine. Every now and then our local papers reported a rash of partridge suicides. The birds crashed through windows or power-dived into buildings or even cracked up against trees. Some years the moose rampage constituted such a hazard on Maine highways that state agencies and the newspapers released bulletins telling motorists how to react if confronted by an antagonistic bull on a dark night. (In recent years as many as 700 moose have been killed annually on Maine highways by colliding with vehicles. Due to the animals' size—up to a half-ton—this usually results in demolished vehicles, serious injuries, and several human fatalities.)

⚬⚬⚬⟩⟨⚬⚬⚬

One of the delightful things about living so close to these wild-woods neighbors of ours was that none of them had a stereotyped behavior pattern. We never knew, as we stepped through our camp door, what strange spectacle would greet us.

Sometimes we speculated on the motivations behind the strange antics of the forest fauna. What forces caused these creatures to "slip their tethers" of normal behavior and suddenly go off on wild sprees? Occasionally, the answer was obvious: The bull moose's annual fall rampage is associated with his mating ritual. At times, though, as in the case of the suicides among partridges, animals' motives defied analysis.

Take the case of the crazy warbler. One day a male myrtle warbler began fluttering wildly against our living-room window, pecking at the pane with his beak. My wife Anita tried all sorts of ruses to get rid of him, but the best she could do was to drive him away temporarily. He was back at the window every day for two weeks before disappearing, inexplicably, for good.

Although I don't profess to any knowledge of bird psychology, I do have a theory. The frenzy seized that bird in the spring, which is mating time for most migratory birds. Many animals, including birds, are extremely aggressive at this time. My guess is that this one saw his reflection in the window, took it for a rival, and accepted the challenge.

The Native Americans called October the "Mad Moon" because of the way animals behaved during that month. Maddest of all must have been the largest beast in the Northeast forest, the moose.

Late September and early October is the moose's mating, or rutting, season. Since early spring the male has been preparing for it, and throughout the summer he concentrates on building up muscle, fat, and stamina. At the same time his body undergoes other changes. The sockets behind his ears become tender, and soon nubbins of antlers begin growing there. When the antlers reach maturity in late summer, the blood supply is cut off and they harden, much as a tree dries up and hardens without its nourishing supply of sap.

By then the moose has already felt the first intimation of madness. During his hour of glory, he will be a demoniacal warrior, and as does every good warrior, he tests his weapons. The velvet has been rubbed from his antlers, the broad palms polished and tines sharpened on brush and trees. Now he stages sham battles with clumps of bushes, and as he grows in confidence (and belligerence), he tackles bigger game. He slams those murderous antlers against full-grown trees, knocking off great slabs of bark and whole limbs, striking terror into the hearts of smaller animals.

When frost whitens the ground the bull moose is ready to venture forth in search of love and combat. By this time a prime specimen weighs in at about half a ton, carries a lethal set of antlers spanning up to six feet in width, measures better than seven feet at the shoulder, and packs enough wallop in a front hoof to break the back of a full-grown horse. During those few weeks of the rut he is as formidable a creature as roams the continent. And to the cow moose, sex appeal is synonymous with brute power, noise, and pugnacity.

A year almost to the day after that moose and logging truck tangled, and less than half a mile away, another big bull was prowling along the Canadian Pacific's right-of-way when a locomotive pulling a string of loaded boxcars came wailing around the bend. Apparently the moose saw it as a monstrous rival. Answering the same blind instinct that seemed to motivate the warbler, he charged down the track straight into the single glaring headlight. I didn't see the result of that encounter, but a trainman told me: "All we ever found of that big fellow was some hamburg."

One fall the bus that carries students from the little community of Rockwood to the high school in Greenville, twenty-five miles away at the southern tip of Moosehead Lake, had to stop half a dozen times because of an aggressive moose. That same season a party of fishermen, driving to camp, discreetly followed a large, snorting bull for seven tense miles one night before he finally plunged into the woods and allowed them to pass. Fortunately, the drivers in both of these instances were acquainted with moose behavior and knew enough not to antagonize a bull in rut. If they had decided to speed up, crowd the moose, blow the horn, or try to pass, the collision would probably have been a loud one.

Such encounters are by no means limited to the northern, sparsely settled part of the state. One road that can rack up a number of moose/vehicle collisions is the Maine Turnpike/ I-95, which knifes through the centers of population. Possessed by the madness of the rut, a moose doesn't always wreak havoc on the roadways; it may just take a notion to visit man's habitat. Every Maine town and city has its local store of moose stories—even the largest, Portland, where almost every year a moose takes a stroll through the business district and often ends up wading in the harbor—to the delight of office workers who hang out of office windows and line the docks, watching.

This usually results in calling out the local police force, game wardens, and biologists, who are led on a merry chase down busy streets and back alleys as they attempt to get close enough to the confused, sometimes panicked animal to shoot it with a tranquilizer dart and truck it back to the woods. One such attempt backfired when the darted animal could not be recovered in time and drowned in the harbor.

Moose have ended up in other strange places. One young bull entered the capital city of Augusta by crossing a high bridge over the Kennebec River. After snacking in the garden behind the governor's mansion, he gave pursuers a wild chase through downtown Augusta, even jumping over the hood of an automobile, before being shot with a tranquilizer and eventually being released in the woods a few miles away. Another bull crashed into a septic tank behind a residence, requiring a crew with a wrecker to raise the smelly animal from its unsavory bath and releasing it.

It would seem that scarcely any creature is immune to the mental derangement engendered by the courting season. Even that sly old devil, Br'er Fox himself, is susceptible, as Anita and I could testify. One wintry afternoon we were in our ice-fishing shanty out on the frozen lake, preparing to return to camp, when I noticed our cocker spaniel, Rusty, sitting immobile at the door and gazing intently down the shore. Following her line of sight, I spotted a pair of foxes moseying along in the direction of our cabin.

This was early February, the start of the mating season for foxes. As we watched, the fox bringing up the rear—obviously the male—attempted to press his affections on his mate. But she wasn't sharing his emotions at the moment, and turned her head to snap at him. Twice more he made passes at her and was repulsed.

As they approached our snowshoe trail I watched them closely, curious to see how they would react to the fresh scent of two humans and a dog. But these foxes were old neighbors of ours and, having run across our scent many times, seemed to know we were friendly. They sniffed along the trail, then disappeared into a strip of woods that runs down the shore a few yards from our cabin.

Rusty hadn't taken her gaze off them. She hopped to her feet the moment they were out of sight and raced pell-mell up the snowshoe track for home—obviously afraid they'd find her buried bones.

Anita and I loaded our ice-fishing gear on the moose sled. Then, while we were lashing on our snowshoes and I was getting into the sled harness, I noticed that one of the foxes had emerged from the woods about a quarter of a mile down the shore and was watching us from the top of a snowdrift. It sat there as we started walking in, then jumped up and began trotting toward us.

In the meantime, Rusty, having satisfied herself that the foxes hadn't disturbed any of her treasures, started back along the trail to meet us and escort us home. So far she wasn't aware that one of the foxes had returned. As we plodded our snowshoe trace, things were becoming interesting, if not tense. Out on that windswept, once-lonely ice (now showing signs of congestion), it seemed as if we were a magnet toward which Rusty and the fox were inexorably being drawn.

When the fox was a hundred feet or so from us I glanced over at Rusty and realized that the two animals were almost certain to meet us at the same moment. By the time the fox reached the fifty-foot mark I was really uneasy. In all my years of rambling through the woods I had never been in a situation quite like this, and I was haunted by vague recollections of newspaper accounts of rabid foxes attacking humans. Could the disease have found its way up here to the Maine woods? I didn't know. But as the fox continued straight toward us, I shrugged out of the harness and stepped back alongside the sled, ready to grab the ice chisel. No telling what would happen.

The fox was no more than twenty-five feet from us when Rusty raised her head and spotted him. Giving a bloodcurdling howl, she made a beeline for him through the soft, powdery snow. The fox stopped dead-still, then wheeled and started back the way he'd come, floating over the snow like a piece of windblown thistledown. Rusty was in close pursuit. We watched until they vanished into the woods, the fox staying just a few yards ahead of the much heavier spaniel and repeatedly looking back at her as the dog floundered and bobbed in his wake.

What could have prompted the traditionally shy, wily fox to approach so close to two humans, a dog, and a large sled in broad daylight? My guess is that, caught in the heat of passion, with his mate not yet receptive to his advances, his brain was addled by the universal madness of frustrated love.

Birds of a Feather

The actions of fox, moose, and warbler seem to be manifestations of unrequited passion, but how to explain the partridge
that committed suicide by crashing through my neighbor's
window? (Her husband replaced the broken pane, and they had
the partridge for supper that night.)

As I've said, this was not a unique occurrence; some years
similar cases are reported throughout the state. I know of one
instance in which a grouse smashed into the window of a
service station located in the center of a large city in southern
Maine.

One weird thing about this occasional mass mania for
suicide among the partridge population (or grouse, if you
prefer—up here they're called simply "bi'ds") is that it doesn't
follow any pattern. Some years we don't hear of a single suicide.
Other years the papers are full of them, and everyone you meet
has had a personal experience which they'll relate at the drop
of a feather. Moreover, the suicides always take place in the fall,
which rules out the sex angle. These birds mate in the spring.

An acquaintance once told me he thought the birds crashed
into windows because the glass is invisible to them, or reflects
the nearby forest, and they believe they can fly right through
it. This might be a tenable theory except that it doesn't explain
why they also fly into solid buildings and trees. Or why these
incidents occur in bunches at the same time of the year.

One of my friends has an idea that, accurate or not, is certainly intriguing. He theorizes that the birds get intoxicated.
If this sounds far-fetched, just hear him out. He reasons that
the partridge's diet is chiefly composed of buds and berries. As
everyone knows, wild crops are cyclical. For example, some
seasons have quantities of beechnuts; other seasons, the beech
trees are almost barren.

He believes that one of the berries that grow in the woods is an intoxicant, at least to partridges. This would explain why they are afflicted only for a few weeks, and always in the fall. That's when the berries reach the peak of ripeness or fermentation. It also explains why the phenomenon doesn't occur every fall, for it would naturally coincide with peak crop years.

What's my opinion? Frankly, I don't know. But I'm afraid that if an intoxicating berry does exist, and if it's equally intoxicating to humans, it will prove disastrous to some of my woodchopper friends. They'll never get out of the woods alive if they find that berry. They won't be able to see the forest for the trees.

In addition to sex and (maybe) intoxication, hunger sometimes drives animals into brief paroxysms of lunatic behavior. My brother Gene became convinced of this after one particular visit with us, for a weekend of fishing.

An avid fisherman, Gene stopped his car by our cabin, dived into the trunk for his gear, and made for the lake. In almost less time than it takes to tell it, he scrambled onto a big boulder that juts out into the water, assembled his rod, and tied on a fly. It was a beautiful afternoon; a large school of trout had moved in close to shore and, aside from the splashes as they fed on a hatch of flies, the lake lay glassy calm.

The ripples had scarcely died around his fly on the first cast when Gene got a savage strike. He set the hook, expertly played the fish out, and soon was depositing a brilliant-hued, foot-long trout on the rock beside him. Again he cast, and within minutes another trout was lying by the first. Gene got excited. This was fishing!

He made a third cast and let out a whoop of joy when another trout slashed at it. In his excitement, he stiff-heeled the fish in and horsed it onto the gravel beach behind him, where it promptly jumped off the hook and started flopping around. He put his rod down and was just starting to climb from the boulder when a big, coal-black mink lunged out from under a pile of driftwood, snatched the struggling trout, and scuttled back to cover.

I was in the house when I heard Gene's howl of dismay. I went out to see what ailed him and got there in time to see him doing an impromptu dance on the boulder, taking wild swipes with his rod butt and screaming curses at an unseen assailant.

"What's the matter—you gone nuts?" I yelled.

"No!" he roared. "But this damn mink has!"

He went into his jumping routine again and took a few more swipes before continuing: "He just stole one of my trout, and now he wants the rest of 'em!"

Gene, a former Marine, stood over six feet tall, weighed in at about 180 pounds, and won quite a few amateur boxing bouts while in the service. The mink, on the other hand, measured a maximum of twenty inches from nose to tail and probably tipped the scales at two and a half pounds.

During the next few minutes pandemonium reigned supreme on that spot of sun-drenched beach. Every few seconds the mink popped out of his hole and tried to scale the heights of Gene's boulder. Gene, in true leatherneck fashion, immediately yelled at the mink and, using his rod butt, thrust and parried in his best bayoneting form.

He finally gave up in disgust, picked up his two trout and gear, and stalked down the beach to another spot. The mink retired to its pile of driftwood and presumably enjoyed its hard-earned dinner. Meanwhile, the school of trout had moved out, and Gene didn't get another catch all day.

On rare occasions, one of Mother Nature's creatures apparently does an illogical thing simply on sheer impulse. Anita and I—and especially Rusty—were fortunate enough to witness such an unpremeditated act one winter.

A local species that provided us endless hours of entertainment was the flying squirrel. It didn't take these elusive little nocturnal creatures long to discover the bonanza of our bird-feeding station, with its never-ending variety of chow. Anita, who was fascinated by all forms of wildlife, kept the feeder well stocked, and soon they were almost nightly visitors.

Unlike their suspicious, daytime-roaming cousins, the red squirrels, flying squirrels have little fear of man. There are few hunters to bother them in the woods at night, and they can glide from tree to tree, high and safe. It wasn't long before Anita had them literally eating out of her hand.

This chumminess was naturally intolerable to Rusty. She dedicated her life to "protecting" us from the multitude of forest denizens that flew or walked over our property, a staggering undertaking for so small a dog. And I strongly suspected that jealousy was involved; Rusty felt the squirrels were stealing Anita's affection.

Rusty kept a close eye on the activities at the feeding station, located at the living-room window, by climbing onto our end table, via the couch, and peering out the window. On that winter night, Anita had the window open and was coaxing a squirrel into taking a morsel from her fingers. Rusty was at her post on the table, nose quivering with the scent of the enemy, and occasionally whining in frustration. The squirrel, meanwhile, sat eating, its back to dog and mistress, tail curved disdainfully over its back.

On impulse, Anita reached out and stroked the luxuriant fur on the little critter's oddly shaped tail. It continued eating as though there weren't another soul around. Anita withdrew her hand and was stepping back from the window when the squirrel spun around and looked intently into the room for a couple of seconds. Then, almost faster than the eye could follow, it launched itself and landed squarely on top of Rusty's nose. In the same instant it whirled and leapt back onto the feeder and resumed eating as though nothing had happened.

Rusty went berserk. We had all we could do to keep her from jumping through the window.

Why did that squirrel do it? Your guess is as good as mine. I think even Rusty—a seasoned, woods-wise dog—was completely mystified.

An earlier version of this story appeared in
Guns & Hunting (May 1961).

9

To Net a Poacher

How Two Illegal Hunters Got Their Bell Rung

A YOUNG MAINE GAME WARDEN literally "rang the bell" on two nonresident hunters in the predawn darkness during the 1972 fall hunting season, catching them in their own deer trap.

The pair, a father and his teenage son from Rhode Island, was convicted in Belfast District Court on several charges of night-hunting and snaring. They pleaded guilty and paid fines totaling $900.

Warden John Ford of Burnham, then twenty-five, learned of the illegal deer trap from three young hunters from the Troy-Unity area who discovered it while hunting in a remote wooded area of Troy. The hunters led Ford through the woods to the trap, which was located in thick woods, some ninety yards from the Rhode Islanders' hidden hunting cabin.

Upon examining the trap, Ford discovered that it had been rigged with a "warning system" to let the trappers know if a catch was made during the night. A monofilament fishing line had been strung from the trap's trigger through eye hooks in trees leading up to the kitchen window of the camp. A tin can filled with stones was tied to the end of the fish line so that it

71

would drop into the
sink when the trap
was tripped.

"They designed
that trap apparently
after seeing too many
Tarzan, jungle-type
movies," Ford said. It
consisted of a heavy
rope cargo net spread
on the ground, con-
cealed with leaves,
and baited with
grain. An elaborate
system of ropes and
pulleys led from
the net to a heavy
boulder resting on a
hinged platform high
up on a tree.

"The theory was
that the deer feeding

Photo courtesy of John Ford Sr.

A fish line ran in through the camp's kitchen window, attached to a soda can filled with nuts and bolts. This served as an alarm to those inside that the trap had been sprung.

on the grain would trip the platform, allowing the rock to fall
and then pulling the net up to snare the deer," Ford explained.
"Meanwhile, the tin can would be released to fall into the
kitchen sink, alerting the hunters of their catch."

Ford, an enterprising young warden who in recent weeks
had taken a new bride, spent a cold, stormy night watching the
trap while the poachers slept in their snug cabin.

At four a.m., Warden Ford brought the camp to life by tripping the alarm.

"The system worked perfectly," he reported. Ford helped to deceive the poachers by crackling the brush and making the bleating sounds of a young deer in distress.

The hunters—one still wearing pajamas—came running out with flashlights and a loaded rifle. Instead of a snared deer, they found the warden waiting with a court summons.

There were a few tense moments as Ford confronted the armed, startled, and angry would-be deer trappers, but they soon surrendered their weapon and were placed under arrest.

In the Belfast court the following morning, the elder hunter was fined $200 for night-hunting and $500 for illegal snaring. The son was fined $200 for the snaring incident, but another fine of $200 for night-hunting was suspended.

The incident was not without its lighter overtones. The Rhode Islanders developed a liking for their warden apprehender. After paying their fines, they invited Ford out for coffee, and even managed a few jokes about their predawn surprise.

Warden Ford then returned to his risky job of protecting Maine's deer herd from meat- and trophy-hungry poachers. The Rhode Islanders returned home, poorer but wiser. Their abortive attempt at illegal hunting had been costly. Not only did their checkbook receive a staggering blow, but they also lost the privilege of hunting in Maine for one year. They could have come the next year to fish . . . but one of them would have had to replace the ninety yards of monofilament line that had helped to ring the bell on them.

An earlier version of this story appeared in
Maine Fish and Wildlife (Winter 1972–73).

10

Can Animals Talk?

Many Animals—Even Insects—Communicate Very Well Indeed

ONE DAY IN THE FALL my brother Gene and I, gliding silently
down a northern Maine stream in a canoe, came unexpectedly
upon a woods family: mama bear and her two cubs. As soon
as she spotted us, Mrs. Bear went into action. Whirling, she
slapped the youngsters to attention. Then she turned around
and faced us again and began grunting.

Behind her the cubs, still playful but knowing better than to
argue with mama, scrambled over to a nearby spruce tree and
started climbing. The sow, continuing to grunt, stayed at her
post until the cubs were near the tree's top. Then, with surprising grace for an animal so large, she clawed her way up the tree
behind the youngsters.

With her young charges safely out of harm's way, the bear
turned to face us once more. Now she began "whistling"—
expelling a series of long, drawn-out sighs, audible mostly as
a high-pitched, whistling sound. Finally she let us know what
she really thought of us. Opening her massive, powerful jaws,
she began loudly gnashing her teeth. The language may have
been foreign, but Gene and I read her message loud and clear:

"Come closer at your peril!" She was still glaring down at us as we paddled away around the next bend and out of sight.

That mother was using common "bear talk." The grunts are standard mom-to-cub lingo for "Get up that tree quick!" The warning is usually accentuated by a stinging cuff behind the ear.

"Whistling" and tooth-popping are manifestations of an angry or annoyed bruin. Bluffing? Perhaps. But it's certainly effective. I've unexpectedly been confronted by those utterances on a dark night. If there is a more blood-chilling sound in nature, I've yet to hear it.

The language of animals has fascinated humans since time immemorial. Interpreting the various methods of communication employed by wildlife was an art well mastered by primitive man, particularly hunters who lured birds and animals by imitating their calls. Later, as man became more civilized, much of this ancient lore was lost or became distorted through misinterpretation. In recent years, however, thanks to the exhaustive research of scientists and the tireless observations of naturalists, man's knowledge of the other creatures that inhabit the Earth has been vastly enriched.

For countless generations, young lovers, romanticists, and poets have rejoiced at the spring song of birds. But it wasn't until the early twentieth century that an English ornithologist named H. Eliot Howard looked into the matter with the detachment of a scientist. He found that the lilting tones of a male bird's spring songs are actually a warning to other males to keep away from his territory.

Not all birds use song to proclaim their territorial rights. One spring day my wife Anita and I were puzzled by a sporadic, metallic clattering near our Maine woods cabin. We prowled and snooped and finally zeroed in on the offender—a brilliantly plumaged, yellow-bellied sapsucker (a member of the woodpecker clan), hammering away at a metal Forest Service sign tacked to a tree behind our woodshed.

During the ensuing weeks, as the mating season came to its peak, that bird's hammering became more and more persistent, and he broadened his activities to tap away at any metallic object he found around camp—tools, tin cans, garbage cans, stovepipe. His crowning achievement was locating an empty oil drum, which responded to his hammering with what must have been an ego-boosting resonance. Then, at the end of the courtship season, the racket stopped, though the bird remained nearby all summer.

Another bird that utilizes sound other than song in its courtship is the ruffed grouse. Early in the spring the grouse selects his drum, usually a large hollow log lying on the ground deep in the woods, on which to do his drumming. Contrary to popular belief, however, the sound isn't caused by the grouse's wings beating on the log. High-speed photographs have shown that the sound is produced by the rapidly moving wings striking the air, much as sound is produced by the flailing blades of an aircraft propeller. The drumming ostensibly serves the same purpose as the songbirds' lilting melodies: to warn away other males and attract amorous females.

<hr/>

Animal communication isn't confined to sound alone. Some animals appear to have their own "written language." Bears maintain "bear trees." Reaching up as high as possible while standing on their hind legs, the bruins mark the tree by scratching the bark with teeth and claws. Their purpose has never been scientifically determined, but it's generally believed to have some significance during the mating season, and to serve as a boundary marker for the bear's home range.

The sense of smell plays an indispensable role in animals' social behaviors. Scent is not only essential in locating food and detecting the presence of enemies, but it's also used by many forms of wildlife as a means of communication. Most of the mustelids, the scent gland–carrying animals, keep track of each other by depositing scent along their regular routes or territorial boundaries. Canines communicate by marking bushes and posts with urine.

Scent also plays a major role in the sex lives of many creatures. Receptive females of many species, including skunks, lure amorous swains from astonishing distances by the emission of various odors. The females in our own society, who often use exotic perfumes effectively, don't have a thing on their wilderness counterparts.

Some of the most bizarre and highly developed communication systems, aside from man's, are found in the insect world. Ant and bee colonies, for instance, are marvelously complex and smoothly efficient social organizations. As vital as a heartbeat to the life of the community is the relaying of information between individuals.

Ants in a colony "talk" to each other through bodily and antennal contact, and by "scent-tasting" the colony's own chemical odor. An ant from a strange colony attempting to enter the nest is immediately recognized as a foreigner and swiftly attacked and killed. Foraging ants commonly follow trails saturated with direction-giving chemicals on their trips to and from the nest.

Probably the nearest thing to talk in the abstract way we use the word is found among the honeybees. Observers have long wondered how a worker bee, stumbling onto a rich food source and returning to its hive, was shortly followed to the spot by swarms of other nectar gatherers. It took a lifetime of pains-taking study by a German scientist, animal behaviorist Karl von Frisch, to work out the puzzle. He found that an excited foraging bee, on returning to the hive, executes a complicated maneuver called the "waggle dance." As other bees excitedly crowd around it, the bee repeatedly makes a series of figure eights, stopping momentarily to waggle its abdomen sideways.

The direction in which the bee faces while "wagging" tells its fellow workers which way the food lies; its dancing speed tells them how far it is. What's more, von Frisch found that a bee sometimes pinpoints food by marking it with a powerful chemical scent.

✦

Late one day in the fall a friend and I were driving along a woods road in northern Maine when we scared up a couple of deer. As they leapt away my companion—an ex-Westerner from the mule deer country of Idaho, who had never seen our Virginia white-tailed deer—exclaimed over the stark whiteness of their erectly waving white tails, or flags.

I explained to him that deer, by hoisting their tails to expose their white underparts and rumps, are flashing an alarm signal to each other. He informed me that the elk in his native Rocky Mountains have a similar white rump patch, which they use in signaling alarm. Mule deer also have an alarm-giving rump patch, but their small, dark tails make it look ludicrous in comparison with the whitetail's. I recalled that when I had spent some time on the plains of eastern Colorado and Wyoming, I'd often seen antelope signaling in this manner. The pronghorns flash danger by erecting their white rump hair, and with their telescopic eyes they can pick up this alarm for miles on the open plains.

Animals' alarm signals often have a universal language. Hunters who have had their presence discovered by such self-appointed forest sentinels as crows, jays, and squirrels know these creatures' cries not only alert members of their own clans, but other forest dwellers as well, including the hunter's quarry. Sometimes, though, this universality backfires. Stealthy hunters have been attracted to game by the jeers and cries of woods spies.

Insects also have methods of sounding the alarm. Social insects alert an entire colony when it is threatened. Excited termites knock their heads against the wooden sides of their nest, which sets up a vibration and arouses the other members of the sensitive colony.

Similarly, some carpenter ants convey the threat of imminent danger by rattling their abdomens against the floor. And, of course, when a beehive is disturbed, its normal drowsy buzzing is suddenly transformed into an angry roar. This generally serves to rout all but the most brazen of interlopers—say, a honey-stealing bear.

Since primitive times, man has been attempting to communicate with animals in their own language, with varying degrees of success. For a long time, the most successful "talkers" have been the hunters, who have long been using various calls and cries to lure game. Squirrel hunters call up the wily nut-stealers by striking and rubbing a couple of half-dollars together which, when executed expertly, closely imitates the squirrels' chattering. Crow and duck hunters use lung-powered calls to attract birds within range of their guns. Absolute mastery of the game-calling

Photo courtesy of Diane Reynolds

V. Paul Reynolds talking moose talk at Ross Stream.

art is required by hunters who toll in wild turkeys and geese.

One of the most thrilling wilderness dramas I've ever witnessed was a French-Indian guide "talking in" a flock of wary honkers to his stool of decoys. From the time he first spotted the birds as mere specks on the horizon and turned them with his blasting "hail" call, through their wide but ever-lowering and tightening circles as they suspiciously scanned his decoy setup, they were lulled into a false sense of security by his reassuring "feeding chuckle" and soon flared in among his decoys. That man's voice guided the flock's every move with the sure mastery of a puppeteer over his dolls.

Among big-game hunters, calling has been mainly practiced by elk hunters, with their bugling calls, and moose stalkers, who use crude, birch-bark horns to imitate a rut-maddened bull's challenge or a cow's plaintive appeal for company. The high degree of accuracy attainable in this type of calling is best exemplified by the tales of the legendary Maine guide who did his expert moose calling only from the protection of a circle of well-armed hunters. He claimed that his rendition of a love-sick cow's wails was so alluring to the bulls that, unless so protected, *he* was in danger.

—⊱✕⊰—

Modern technology has begun breaking the man–wild-life language barrier. Scientists have recorded bird calls, and by replaying them over and over and transmitting the sound through an oscillograph to reproduce its "picture," they have been able to study subtle differences and nuances that are undiscernible to the human ear. From these studies scientists have developed complex electronic game calls, some so effective that their use by hunters has been outlawed in some states.

One of the most notable achievements in this field was the pioneering work done in ridding areas of our exploding starling population. After years of trying poisons, loud noises, electric shocks, explosives, and just about everything else short of black magic—without success—officials were about to give up.

Then Professor Hubert Frings of Penn State University discovered the starlings' Achilles' heel: They can't stand the sound of another starling's distress screeches. By recording the screeches and then, with a sound truck, going to their roosts and replaying them at ear-piercing volume, Professor Frings and his associates were able to drive away the overabundant star-lings from certain areas, sometimes for good.

These kinds of breakthroughs offered unfathomable pos-sibilities in man's never-ending quest for the key to unlocking nature's secrets. Science now knows that animals do "talk"—and that when their language is learned, people can talk to them.

An earlier version of this essay appeared in *Field
& Stream* magazine (June 1964).

Part 2:
Water-Bound

11

Land of the Landlocks

The Poor Man's Aristocrat of Fishdom

WHEN YOU THINK of salmon fishing it conjures up images of the aristocrat of game fishes: the Atlantic salmon, *Salmo salar*. The species is federally listed as endangered on all Maine rivers from the Androscoggin east, which means that angling for this piscatorial sophisticate usually means going to exclusive, expensive clubs and remote rivers in places like Labrador, Newfoundland, Ireland, or Scotland. Which means: Bring money.

But fortunately for those of us less endowed with riches, the Atlantic salmon has a poorer country cousin, if you will, that can provide most of the thrills of salmon angling closer to home: the landlocked salmon.

Maine is where landlocks originated, and the state still provides the most opportunities for making their acquaintance. Best of all, the muscular gamester is accessible to anglers of modest means.

One of the first landlocked salmon I ever caught came from one of the unlikeliest bodies of water—Little Parker Pond in Jay, Maine, where I was born and raised.

As Maine waters go, the pond is rather nondescript. It's small, weed-grown, and muddy-bottomed. Muskrats swim its swampy outlet, moose and deer feed on its aquatic plants, and pugnacious pickerel and smallmouth bass stalk its weed patches. The latter were what had brought me, a gangling teenager with a battered casting rod, to probe its waters from a silent-gliding canoe.

The pond was, as usual, deserted. No camps marred its shores. The murky waters held little attraction to water-sports enthusiasts in a state so richly endowed with clear blue lakes.

But something about Parker's neglected seclusion appealed to me—and occasionally draws me still.

On this particular late-September day, the attraction was the pond's population of smallmouths. This, too, was odd behavior for a Mainer. The bass was then considered a "trash" fish, but I was a small-town lad, too naive and ignorant to know better. I just kept returning to Parker and challenging its tackle-smashing bass and having a ball.

But on this day Parker would reveal one of her secrets. As my canoe glided in toward the landing, I decided to try one more cast of my topwater bass lure as I passed the pond's main tributary stream. My jitterbug had barely plopped into the water under an overhanging alder when it was hit by a slashing strike.

This was no sagging-paunched bass. Smallmouths are occasional jumpers, but this fish made a dazzling series of rapier-like thrusts into the air. Barely would it touch the water before it was up again, flashing silver in the sunlight. Definitely not a bronzeback bass. But what was it?

In my surprise I failed to pull the slack out of the line, and in minutes the fish had wrapped itself up with several turns of line. I brought it aboard and gazed in amazement at a landlocked salmon. Thin, racy, two and a half pounds of silver lightning.

I would later learn from longtime area residents that years before, some hopeful angler had dumped a pailful of salmon fry into Parker's unlikely waters. A small population somehow managed to survive the pond's atypical salmon habitat as well as the predatory pickerel and bass, and continued to propagate naturally.

One of the landlocked salmon's greatest attributes is that it can survive under rather tough environmental conditions. Its classy first cousin, the seagoing Atlantic salmon, has drastically declined over the years and is today available primarily to wealthy members of exclusive clubs which own fishing rights on certain rivers in Canada and Northern Europe (though some sea-run Atlantics are still caught each year on several coastal rivers in eastern Maine, under limited catch/release regulations.) The landlock's range, meanwhile, has expanded.

How did this salmon come to be "landlocked"? Fishing camps and scientists' ivory towers have rung with arguments on this subject for more than a century. An early theory claimed they were sea-run salmon that had become trapped in freshwater by man-made dams or natural obstructions to migration. Another theory said they originated in freshwater as a species apart from the sea salmon.

The accepted scientific opinion today is that the landlocked salmon originated from the sea-run salmon, through physiological adaptation and heredity brought on by thousands of years of changing conditions in the glacial lakes of the northeastern American continent.

Scientists now say they can find no morphological differences between the landlocks and the sea salmon; in fact, they share the species name. They are also close kin to a similar species, the *ouananiche*, found in some waters in eastern Canada.

Whatever the scientific explanation, these Maine natives love clean freshwater and refuse to go to sea even when they have ready access to it. This is all to the good for sportfishermen.

One of the main drawbacks to successful Atlantic salmon management is that the fish spend much of their adult lives at sea, unavailable to sportfishing and under heavy exploitation by predators and commercial fishermen. Landlocks, on the other hand, remain loyal to their home waters and are available throughout the year during open seasons, even in winter under the ice.

Maine landlocks were originally found in four major river systems in the state, where they provided food and sport to the original Native American inhabitants (the Passamaquoddy Indians of eastern Maine called the landlock *Tagewahnahn*) and the early European settlers. The river basins and their connected lake and pond systems were the Presumpscot (including Sebago Lake, which became world-renowned for offering up the world-record landlock), the Penobscot, the Union, and the St. Croix of eastern Maine, including popular East and West Grand lakes.

Over a century ago, anglers who had learned to love this Maine sport fish attempted to bring it to other parts of the country. Scientists believe the first artificial stocking of land-locked salmon occurred in 1868, when 800 salmon eggs from Grand Lake Stream were planted at Cathance Lake in Washington County.

From 1874 to 1880, Maine landlocked salmon were introduced into waters in twenty-two states, from New England to California and south to the Carolinas. But most of these were doomed to failure because of inadequate water quality and spawning areas. Today, some waters in the states of New Hampshire, Vermont, and New York have salmon fisheries maintained by stocking programs. Curiously, one of the most successful transplantings was to waters in Argentina and Chile.

But the deep, cold waters of Maine remain the primary domain of the landlocked salmon. The Maine Department of Inland Fisheries and Wildlife now lists 303 Maine lakes known to contain salmon populations; 75 percent of these sustain good populations through natural spawning. Artificial stocking and good management account for the salmon populations in the other Maine lakes.

It has been my good fortune during the past few decades to have fished many of Maine's better landlocked waters. I spent a number of my youthful years as a fishing guide, bush pilot, and camp operator in the Moosehead Lake region—Maine's largest and best-known salmon water. I like to think that I learned a little about the salmon's habits and how to catch them. But any glow of pride must be tempered by the knowledge that the salmon is a good-hitting fish and not too difficult to catch, most of the time. Fortunate for me, else my career would have been shortened.

In the spring, just after ice-out, salmon come to the surface and prowl the mouths of rivers and streams for smelts, their favorite prey. That's the best time to fish for them. The two most popular springtime salmon baits are streamer flies (such as the Nine-Three; Warden's Worry; Grey, Green, and Black Ghosts; Supervisor; Mickey Finn; and even the gaudy Montreal Whore, all designed to resemble a swimming smelt), or a sewed smelt on a snelled hook. The flies can be either cast or trolled behind a boat or canoe.

Many springtime salmon anglers like to troll their flies or sewed smelts at a lively clip—say 6 to 10 mph—and on a short line. Some troll the bait only a few feet behind the boat so that it swirls within the frothing propeller wash. One fishing pal of mine, Herb McIntire (who also happens to be one of coastal Maine's top tuna boat skippers), thinks that the turbulent prop wash resembles the white bellies of fleeing forage fish and triggers the salmon's feeding instinct. Whatever the reason, it works.

As the season progresses and the sun warms the waters, salmon leave the surface and seek deep, colder levels. During much of early summer they can be caught by trolling streamers or sewed bait at depths of from five to twenty feet or so below the surface.

In July and through August, warming surface waters may send them down to depths ranging from fifteen to seventy feet. At whatever depth, salmon are seldom far from their favorite forage, smelts. If you hope to catch them, you'll have to fool them with baits and lures that resemble smelts at those depths. Most deepwater salmon trollers tie shiny lures or spoons to their lines in hopes they will attract salmon more readily in the darker depths. A fairly stout boat rod, equipped with a large-capacity reel filled with lead-core multicolored line, is the most popular gear. Downriggers, which allow deep fishing with lighter tackle, are growing in popularity. Good summer trolling lures are the Mooseluc Wobbler, Weeping Willow, Super-Duper, Rapala, Fjord Spoons, and similar lures.

Salmon aren't supposed to feed on the surface during the summer months, but no one has told the salmon. I recall the August day a sport showed up at my camp on Brassua Lake, informed me that he had never caught a salmon on a dry fly, wanted to, and had only that afternoon in which to do it. I assured him the season was wrong, and it would be well-nigh impossible. He insisted. So we embarked down the shoreline in a canoe while he cast—rather expertly, as I recall—a Silver Doctor.

You guessed it. We hadn't traveled a quarter-mile before a big salmon burst out from under a driftwood tangle and nailed his fly. It weighed some five pounds. Sometimes salmon will come up and feed on insect hatches. Surprised and happy is the dry-fly trout angler who chances upon them.

There are several fine salmon fly-fishing rivers in Maine. Among my favorites are the Rapid River which drains the Richardson Lakes; the Moose, from Jackman to Moosehead Lake; the Kennebago at Rangeley; the upper stretches of the Kennebec, including Moosehead's East Outlet; the Penobscot West Branch above Millinocket; and Grand Lake Stream in extreme eastern Maine. There are others—and I hope to fish more.

One season generally overlooked by much of the angling fraternity is early fall, when salmon again move into the shallows. They enter the mouths of tributaries or outlets in October and November for spawning. Some of the year's best salmon fishing is at the Penobscot River near Chesuncook Lake, Grand Lake Stream, and the Kennebago River near Rangeley. Most Maine rivers remain open until September fifteenth; many have extended fly-fishing-only seasons in the fall.

Even that rugged individualist, the ice fisherman, can enjoy salmon fishing in Maine. Many lakes are open to ice-fishing for salmon and trout in the winter months.

On a windswept, biting-cold day in March a few years ago, I hiked across Moosehead Lake near Kineo Mountain with a couple of biologists from the Maine Department of Inland Fisheries and Wildlife to observe their work checking winter salmon catches. They happily told me that the big lake is making a comeback after several lean fishing years. According to Dave Boucher, Fisheries Management Supervisor at IF&W in Augusta, the salmon fishing in Moosehead has greatly improved since the biologists increased the limit on togue (lake trout) and reduced them from competing with salmon for available food. Today, after a period of ups and downs brought about by fishing pressure, bulldozed spawning streams, and fluctuating water levels, most problems have been solved and the Moosehead salmon are coming back strong.

⬛━✕━⬛

Sebago Lake, north of Portland and its chief water supply, is famous for its salmon population. But during the 1950s, the lake began losing its salmon. One of the leading salmon "managers" at the time, state biologist Stuart DeRoche, was assigned to find out why. After much study he pinpointed the cause: Excessive spraying of DDT by lakeside cottage owners and farmers had created alarming levels of the pesticide in the lake, not only killing aquatic insect life essential to the food chain, but also threatening the health of the population of Portland, which still gets its water from Sebago.

Once he found the culprit, Stu had to convince the sprayers that they were harming the very lake they loved. He told his story at fish and game club meetings, to the press, and through every forum available. His efforts began paying off. Spraying programs were voluntarily discontinued even before DDT was officially banned. Then Stu began working to restore the once-abundant salmon to their native water. Soon he had reestablished smelt runs, and the salmon began to reappear in numbers in Sebago.

On a fall day some years later I stood with Stu on the banks of a major Sebago tributary while his assistants netted salmon to be stripped of their eggs for propagation of salmon in Sebago and other waters. Hundreds of salmon, ranging up to five or six pounds, crowded into the stream, driven by the age-old urge to spawn and perpetuate their kind. They were heavy, healthy, lusty fish—Stu DeRoche's legacy to future Maine anglers.

Maine continues to work hard to preserve the quality of its lakes and rivers to ensure that salmon will be available to future generations. The state has enacted tough environmental laws which control growth and development around lakes and ban the dumping of pollutants into the state's waters. Fishways have been built, and many old dams removed from rivers and streams to permit passage of salmon and trout to spawning areas

The landlocked salmon is well worth these efforts. It's not only a handsome, strong-hearted fighter, but it is also adaptable to living under a fairly wide range of environmental conditions. However, it does need relatively clean, cold, well-oxygenated water—of which Maine fortunately still has an abundance.

Best of all, the salmon is everybody's fish. It is relatively easy to catch, even by the unsophisticated angler. The landlock makes fishing available to all levels of the fishing public—truly the poor man's aristocrat of fishdom.

A version of this essay first appeared in the
1974 *Cord Communications Fishing Annual.*

12

Bigotry in the Big Maine Woods

"Restricted Clientele" Had a Meaning All Its Own

ANTI-SEMITISM WAS A multisyllabic word whose meaning most of us would have had to look up in the small Maine town where I grew up in mid-twentieth-century Maine. Though we were for the most part unaware of it, bigotry and discrimination were, nonetheless, alive and well in some areas of our state. And I, a mere lad emerging from my teens, became for one day unwittingly involved in a strange little drama on one of Maine's most beautiful, remote rivers.

The spring of 1948 for me was, as the song goes, developing as a very good year. At nineteen, I was already a Registered Maine Guide. When the ice left the lakes in May, I was engaged as a fishing guide at a sporting camp in western Maine.

Here was a unique little sportsman's paradise, tucked away in a remote corner of the state close by the New Hampshire and Quebec borders. The Richardson Lakes are the lowest, wildest, and least known of the Rangeley chain of lakes. Most of the land around them was then managed by the Brown Paper Company, which operated a paper mill at Berlin, New Hampshire, and used the forests as a source of wood, employing the lakes and their connecting rivers to drive the pulpwood down to the mill.

It was evidently in the best interests of the company to keep the region wild and undeveloped. There was only one gravel road to the extreme southern shore of Lower Richardson Lake at South Arm. Most of the lake's shoreline was still wild and untouched, with only an occasional primitive fishing cottage sprinkled here and there. Fortunately for this neophyte guide, the waters held sizable populations of trout and landlocked salmon.

The camp was ideally situated to protect its natural wealth. To reach the hotel and cabins required a five-mile ride by boat across Lower Richardson Lake from South Arm. Guests arriving at the camps, and all supplies, were brought in on a forty-foot cabin launch operated by the camp. If you didn't have legitimate business there, you didn't get on the boat.

Since the turn of the twentieth century, the lodge's clientele had capitalized on its remoteness and inaccessibility to create for themselves what amounted to a private retreat, even though the lodge was a commercial venture. It was owned by a couple. The soft-spoken husband was usually found in company with several handymen who assisted him in unloading supplies from the twice-daily boat arrivals, grooming the spacious grounds, maintaining the power generator, and generally keeping up the premises—which included a sizable ancient hotel dining room and a dozen or so log cabins scenically situated overlooking the lake, and where the paying guests lived.

We guides and other single male help had rooms in the guides' camp behind the hotel. Female employees lived in rooms above the kitchen and "back hall," the dining room reserved for hired help and guides.

This situation was ideal for the paying guests, who were pampered and fed as sumptuously as was possible in such a remote location. The original guests early in the century had been members of Boston and New York City's elite—among the wealthiest of America's high society during that era. The current guest list was largely made up of their descendants. The names on the guest register matched those of some of America's most prestigious WASP families and firms, the bluest of American blue bloods. And while it was never openly discussed by the guests—at least, never in my presence—I soon learned from guide camp scuttlebutt that they intended to keep it to themselves.

The first indication came one evening when I was relaxing by the camp stove, browsing through a copy of a national sportsmen's magazine. I chanced upon an advertisement for the camps, and my eyes settled on a line which had previously puzzled me. It read RESTRICTED CLIENTELE.

I held the page up to one of the grizzled old veteran guides and, pointing at the line, asked, "What's this mean?"

He glanced at me with the look he usually reserved for trash fish which had attached themselves to his sports' fishing lines. "Don't you know?" he inquired, in a tone that failed to conceal his contempt at my stupidity.

"Nope."

"It means 'No Jews Allowed!' " he responded emphatically.

Looking further through the magazine's advertising section, I found a number of other lodges carrying the same tagline. Obviously, this was a common practice, but since it had little to do with my busy little world, I soon forgot it.

One of the major distractions in my young life had arrived that spring in the form of a lovely young woman with honey-blonde hair and soft, intriguing, blue-green eyes. Freshly graduated from Rumford High School, she had been hired as the "back-hall girl," i.e., it was her job to serve as our waitress, and to clean up and generally take care of the guides' and other staff's dining room. As such, she also prepared the noon lunch packs and cookouts we guides took out for our guests. This meant I got to spend extra time in her company most days. I began to notice that my meals were being served with a touch more personal attention and smiles than was my norm. Whenever I looked into those eyes, my bony knees turned to Jell-O. I was hooked.

This, then, was the exciting, pleasant way my life was unfolding on a spectacularly bright, sunny June day in 1948. The couple I'd been guiding for the past week had departed for home on the morning boat. Pleased with the week's great fishing success, they'd rewarded me with a generous tip to fatten my wallet. My next fishing party wasn't due in until the following morning. I had a free day, and I was going fishing. (Guides seldom get to fish. They're too busy rigging tackle and handling outboard motors and looking out for the welfare of careless sports and netting others' fish to catch any of their own.)

With the camp boat bearing my party slowly diminishing down the lake, I returned to the back hall and had the soft-eyed girl prepare me a couple of sandwiches, which I tucked into a tackle bag slung over my shoulder. At the guides' camp I picked up a slender, shiny, new split-bamboo fly rod I'd purchased during the winter—and had scarcely yet had an opportunity to try out. My stride was long, my steps light as I followed the path downriver to the next dam in the chain, where I hoped to find some salmon hungry for my flies.

Soon, I was happily perched on a pier on the downstream side of the Pond-in-the-River (shortened to "Pondy River" by all who came there) dam. The new fly rod bent fluidly as it cast the line with its attached leader and dry fly out into the eddies and still pockets among the racing current. The roar of water rushing through the sluice gates drowned out all other sounds. For a pleasantly indeterminate time I was mesmerized—lost in a world of rushing water, gracefully curving rod and line, delicately floating fly . . . and honeyed curls and blue-green eyes.

At length, around midday, this pleasant reverie was rudely interrupted. I became aware of a presence on the shore, seeking my attention. I looked up to see a stranger standing there, motioning to me to come ashore. Irritated but curious, I reeled in the line and balance-skipped my way over the log cribwork to the riverbank.

The person standing before me was a middle-aged stranger—and obviously a sport. He was a bit shorter than average height, a bit on the stout side. If anything, his attire was a bit too "sporty": a gaudy hat covered with flies, a light tan fisherman's jacket with many pockets. A tad flashier than the dark brown or gray tweedy look favored by most of our conservative clientele. But my mind noted these impressions fleetingly. He was, after all, a sport. Few things a sport did or wore ever startled a Maine guide. Sports were *expected* to behave and dress bizarrely.

With a touch of anxiety in his voice, he inquired, "Are you Paul, the guide?"

"A-yup." (Guide etiquette rule #1: When in the presence of sports, always assume the taciturn/rustic stance.)

He looked relieved. "The boat operator said you might be here, and that perhaps I could hire you to help me catch some fish."

I could sense my perfect day being spoiled. "Uh, I don't work half-days."

His round face beamed in a warm, engaging smile. "Oh, I'll be glad to pay you for the full day. The boat man told me you're the best guide around for catching fish!"

Well. This required some rethinking. Stroking a youthful ego can be damned effective. And a full day's guide wages was seven bucks—a not inconsequential sum in 1948 dollars. On top of that morning's generous tip, this was promising to be a remarkably profitable day.

I relented. "Okay." After a few minutes' discussion as to where he wanted to fish, I picked up his rod and a surprisingly large and heavy tackle box, and we walked downstream to some pools I'd been planning to fish anyway.

While we had stood there talking, I looked up above the dam and spotted the local game warden standing there watching us. We exchanged waves. He was an infrequent visitor at the lodge. He obviously knew our clientele were law-abiders, and he never bothered to check us. Sometimes after dinner he'd sit on the camp porch and swap yarns with the older guides. He'd scarcely ever spoken to me, only exchanging pleasantries whenever we met. Now, when I walked past him to deposit my rod and pack at a small shelter near the dam, he asked in a low voice, "Where'd you find that rig?" (*Rig* in Maine parlance can mean any unusual item—or person.) "Oh, he just showed up. Came in on the morning boat, I guess, and wants me to guide him. Why, what's the problem?"

"He's a Jew, and he slipped in on the boat this morning, before anyone spotted him. They'll be waitin' for him at the hotel!"

"Anything wrong with me guiding him?" I inquired.

"Guess not. It's up to you." I shrugged and returned to the riverbank. All sports were the same to me—all strange beings, from alien places.

Later, I would realize that I had overlooked two vital questions I should have asked of my client:

1) *Was he a registered guest at the hotel?* The assumption that he was hadn't been difficult to reach. After all, there was no other way he should have arrived on that boat. And while there was no written agreement, it was understood that if you were staying at a sporting camp, you guided its sports.

2) *Did he have a fishing license?* Of course. No one would go to that expense and distance to go fishing without a relatively inexpensive license. And the super-efficient camp owner would have made sure he had one upon registering, or sold him one on the spot, as they were bona fide Maine Fish and Game license agents, as a convenience for their guests.

Reaching the first pool, I began stringing up his fly rod. I noted that it was an expensive piece from a famous New York City sporting goods emporium. As I ran the line through the guides, he opened up that curious big tackle box I'd lugged down. It was the first I'd seen like it. The box, half the size of a suitcase, opened by splitting apart at the top. As he opened it out wider, I could see that its deep covers pivoted out on both sides. On each side were trays, cleverly attached so that the wider he opened the box, the more layers were revealed. And the trays were crammed with flies and other tackle—enough, it looked to me, to stock a small tackle store.

We gingerly poked among the flies trying to make a choice from the bewildering array. I spotted some of the regular favorites on the river: Silver Doctor, Hare's Ear, Royal Coachman. And many others I didn't recognize.

I selected one of my favorites, a Fanwing Coachman, tied it to the leader, and handed the rod to the man. But he waved me off.

"You fish for a while. I'd like to watch and see how you do it."

I was taken aback. In all of my brief guiding career, I'd never seen a client make his guide do the fishing—especially with the sport's own expensive rod, which was often a revered family heirloom.

"Are you sure?" I asked, confused. But he insisted.

By now I was losing my composure. This was getting curiouser and curiouser.

I shrugged and stepped into the pool. I began stripping out line and false-casting, getting the feel of this finely crafted piece of split bamboo, eyeing and studying the currents to find the choicest locations to present the fly to a hopefully hungry waiting fish.

I began with short casts, working the high-floating fly over the nearer water to make sure no fish were lurking there, and gradually lengthening the casts. This rod and line were a substantial cut above my new $20 fly rod. This was going to be a pleasant way to earn a day's pay.

My casts were just beginning to reach some of the more promising water, up near the head of the pool where an eddy meets the main current—and where big fish are likely to be waiting in the quieter water, watching for food to come drifting by—when the sport shouted from the shore: "Well, that fly's not working too well. Let's change it."

"What? I haven't really given it a good try, yet."

"Let's change it," he insisted, pointing to his cavernous case. "There are some better ones in here."

Well, I thought, he's paying for this, so let's play along. While I cut off the Coachman, he pawed through the trays, picking up one fly after another—a wet, or a dry, or a streamer fly, with neither rhyme nor reason. "How about this one?" Or something like this? Suppose they'd like that?" Once he picked up a huge bass plug, grinning mischievously. I shook my head in annoyance. Why had he lugged all of that heavy junk to a trout and salmon river?

Soon he opened the box to its widest for the first time, so that the bottom compartment was visible. And there was a can full of moist, squirming angle worms. "Here!" he exclaimed, grinning broadly. "This'll get 'em!"

I was indignant. "You can't use those here. This is a fly fishing-only river! You'd better throw those away."

"Oh, no. I might need them later."

By now, even my dull brain had perceived something was amiss here. I asked, "Are you staying at the hotel?"

"No, I just came in for the day."

"Do you have a fishing license?"

"Sure. Why do you ask?"

"I can't guide you unless you've got a license. It's the law." I wanted to cover my butt.

He pulled a license out of his wallet and showed it to me. I didn't catch the name, but could see that it was, indeed, a current State of Maine Nonresident Fishing License. Instead of returning it to his wallet, I noticed that he tucked it in the tackle box under some streamer flies.

I tied another fly on the leader and waded back out into the pool. I was beginning to feel annoyed. What was this guy up to?

I again began casting toward the head of the pool. Somehow, I wasn't surprised when I glanced up and saw the warden standing above us on the riverbank, again watching us. In a few minutes he came slowly down the trail.

Between trying to present the fly as carefully as possible and watching my backcast to keep it from snagging some trees on the shore, I had my hands full. But I strained to hear what was going on between the two men. I caught part of the conversation.

"How come you ain't fishing?"

"Oh, I'd rather watch and see how he does it."

They talked in low tones for a few minutes. Then I saw the sport begin searching through his pockets. That fancy, multi-pocketed jacket gave him ample opportunity to make it as slow and meticulous a search as possible. He opened his wallet and painstakingly went through each compartment. The warden stood by, hands on hips, obviously doing a slow burn. Then the man got down on his knees and began opening that damned tackle box—the one I knew contained his license, and that can of worms. Again, there was an agonizingly laborious search.

It was painfully obvious now, even to this country clod, that this guy was playing a game, having fun at the expense of these yokels. The warden was red-faced, on the verge of exploding. He pulled what I assumed was a summons book and pencil out of his pocket. This was getting serious. No responsible guide wants the black mark of a violation by his client to mar his reputation. I began reeling in and waded ashore.

The sport played his little drama out to the hilt. By now, he had the tackle box opened out to its last layer of trays. One more, and the worm can would be exposed. At the last possible moment, he miraculously found his license and showed it to the game warden.

He studied it carefully and returned it to its owner. He glared at him for a moment. His face was beet red, and a large vein bulged out on his forehead. Then he turned and stalked off up the hill.

I turned to the sport. "What in hell did you do that for?"

"Oh, I just wanted to have a little fun with him!" He grinned.

The man finally took his rod and fished for a short time—casting rather expertly, I noted. Then he paid me my full day's wages, picked up his gear, and with a friendly grin and wave started walking back up the trail toward the hotel and the afternoon boat to take him back to South Arm. I stuffed my seven dollars—plus a tip—into my wallet and went back to Pondy Dam to resume my interrupted fishing

I got back to the hotel that evening just in time for supper, an event I never intentionally missed, to find the back hall buzzing with excitement and everyone waiting to hear from me what had happened. I was told that the warden had come storming up the trail, stopped briefly at the hotel lobby to speak with some guests, and then jumped into his boat and roared off down the lake, obviously boiling mad. Later, when the sport had shown up, he was met and surrounded by a group of camp guests. Heated words were exchanged as he was escorted down to the landing and onto the boat and sent off down the lake.

This was about the greatest excitement any of the hired help had ever seen. As for me, I was busy attending to my supper

(I had a famously prodigious appetite) and basking under the warm smile of the back-hall girl.

Later that evening in the guides' camp, the boat operator (who had obviously been chastened) explained to me. "Hell! He seemed like a nice-enough, friendly guy. How the hell was I to know he wasn't a hotel guest? He just looked like another sport to me!"

⋯⋯⋯

Indeed. To us native Mainers, these out-of-state sports were all strange, with their big shiny automobiles, expensive clothing and equipment, and sharp accents and mannerisms—as exotic to us as would be a giraffe among a herd of moose.

My idyllically simple, happy life at the sporting camp was too good to last. My life took on new directions, new challenges.

Within two years, that lovely back-hall girl had become my wife, and we lived far away from Maine. War clouds were gathering way off in the Far East at a place called Korea. Within a few months of our marriage, I was serving in the US Air Force. It would be four long years before I became a civilian again—years that were lightened only by thoughts of Maine with its beautiful lakes and rivers and mountains.

By the time I returned, the world was changing. Courageous people were taking stands against discrimination and bigotry—even losing their lives for the cause in some cases. In time, this would lead to enlightenment, and ultimately to landmark legislation, culminating in the Civil Rights Act, which ended discrimination that had existed for centuries. The tagline RESTRICTED CLIENTELE disappeared. Under Subchapter 11 of the Maine Statutes relating to Public Accommodations, it is now spelled out: *All persons shall be entitled to the full and equal enjoyment of the goods, services, facilities, privileges, advantages, and accommodations of any place of public accommodation, as defined in this section, without discrimination or segregation on the ground of race, color, religion, or national origin.*

I've never understood what motivated this man to spend a few hours amusing himself by baiting and humiliating a few naive rustics. That analysis I'll leave to the psycho-sleuths. But there's no question that he was a pioneer, likely the first of his ethnic background to crash the exclusive little WASP enclave at Middle Dam and sample the fishing in its pristine waters.

Those waters still flow clean and lovely down the Rapid River, draining the Rangeley chain of lakes into New Hampshire for a brief sojourn before returning to Maine as the Androscoggin River. And anglers of any race, color, religion, or country still come to fish for salmon and trout and, more importantly, to refresh their souls from the rush of life in more harried worlds.

13

The Race to Save Maine's Rarest Trout

Fighting the Extinction of the Arctic Char

AT ONE TIME A FISH NOW RARE in Maine could be found in many of its lakes, and several in New England. Today, among the Lower Forty-Eight, this uncommon trout exists precariously only in Maine waters, and in only twelve of the state's six thousand lakes and ponds.

In one instance, it required herculean efforts, including a helicopter and seaplane airlifts, to rescue the species from being exterminated in one of Maine's most pristine remote ponds.

After years of study and preparation, in June 2011, Igor I. Sikorsky III, grandson of a Russian pilot legendary in aviation history, flew 600 arctic char (aka, blueback, Sunapee, and golden trout) back to their ancestral home at Big Reed Pond in northern Maine.

The seven- to nine-inch-long fish were transported from a hatchery in northern Maine in plastic bags containing chilled water heavily charged with oxygen to keep them healthy and lively.

The plan brought in 300 more char the next fall, 10 of which were implanted with ultrasonic tags to allow scientists to track survival and habitat use throughout the year over a period of three years, according to Frank Frost, fisheries biologist and leader of the project to reclaim the ninety-acre pond.

Sikorsky also flew in nearly 1,500 brook trout fry (only a few months old). These were hand-carried from the pond several miles up tributary streams before being released to reestablish that population. According to Sikorsky, this gave the larger, older char a "leg up" over the brookies. The previous October the state of Maine had "killed" Big Reed, one of its most pristine, isolated wilderness trout ponds, in order to save it.

The operation actually began in September. Chief warden pilot Charlie Later flew loads of lumber strapped to the pontoons of his Cessna 185 to Big Reed Pond for use in constructing a landing dock for receiving supplies at the pond. It took three flights to haul the lumber used to build the twelve-by-twelve-foot platform near the shore.

This stage was necessary because the owners of the surrounding land wished to protect it from disturbance. They stipulated that no trees be cut or clearances made in the virgin timberland. In fact, several bed logs for the dock were salvaged from downed timber and hand-carried to the site. During this period Sikorsky and warden pilot Daryl Gordon flew some eighteen to twenty missions, bringing in generators, boats, motors, nets, and other gear.

Normally, Maine warden pilots would be involved throughout such an operation, but this period in the fall is their busiest season. Moose and other hunting seasons in effect and other regular stocking jobs require their services, so private pilot Sikorsky handled the majority of the day-to-day flying.

Since the Ice Age, Big Reed Pond in the northern Allagash wilderness region of Maine has harbored populations of three species—and three exclusively—of fish that have coexisted harmoniously: northern redbelly dace, brook trout, and, the rarest of all, arctic char. The dace and brook trout are commonly found, but the char are rare gems.

Though populations of char occur globally in the northern climes, none are found below the forty fifth parallel. Maine has the world's southernmost population. In fact, it is the only state in the Lower Forty-Eight to still contain a sustaining population. All of those twelve lakes and ponds are remote or inaccessible.

Located some fifty miles from the nearest settlement, at the center of a nearly 5,000-acre virgin forest refuge owned and zealously guarded by The Nature Conservancy, Big Reed Pond seems invulnerable. It has been visited over the years by relatively few anglers who came by small floatplane or primitive hiking trail to sample its unique fishery. During that period of light fishing, it continued to produce healthy populations of trout and char. That is, until disaster struck in the form of an "alien invasion."

At first glance, arctic char are similar to brookies. They sport flaming orange fins and, especially during the fall spawning time, assume a rich, orange-yellow pigmentation on their sides and bellies. This has earned them the name "golden" trout. While they often share the same waters and similar environmental requirements—clean, cool, well-oxygenated—the brookies (*Salvelinus fontinalis*) occupy the shallower to mid-levels, while the char (*Salvelinus alpinus*) prefer the deeper, cooler depths. The dace, locally called chubs, stay in the shallows and offer little or no space competition.

During the 1990s, those fish populations—especially the char, but also brook trout—declined drastically. From an estimated population of some 600 char in Big Reed in 1993, the estimate dropped down to perhaps fewer than 30 in 2009. Brook trout fared somewhat better, but not much. The culprit? An illegal introduction of rainbow smelts (*Osmerus mordax*) to Big Reed's fragile, vulnerable ecosystem.

In many of Maine's larger trout and salmon lakes, smelts are a major forage fish for the larger game fish, but not in a small, delicately balanced ecosystem populated by two trout species notoriously sensitive to competition. In fact, arctic char are perhaps the least tolerant of all Maine species to competitors. No doubt this is why they've long since disappeared from many waters.

Smelts are extremely fecund breeders, and their population in Big Reed exploded. As they grew, they not only consumed much of the tiny zooplankton upon which young trout rely, but also ate up the young trout hatchlings. They took over.

The smelts most likely reached Big Reed in some fisherman's bait bucket. Whether this was inadvertent dumping by an angler at the end of the day, or a deliberate act of illegal stocking, will never be known.

Some misguided individuals think they can "improve" on nature by bringing in other species. Often, it's to the detriment of the fishery. As at Big Reed, instead of the hoped-for end of providing a new food source—and thus bigger and more trout—the introduction resulted in killing them off.

After numerous meetings between department fishery biologists and other interested parties, it was reluctantly decided to take the drastic step of chemically removing *all* the fish from Big Reed and restocking.

The simple solution would have been to restock from other sources, but that would have meant the loss of the endemic (native to that water body) strains. The genetic uniqueness of the Big Reed strains of both brook and golden trout was considered so valuable that heroics were considered worth the effort.

In 2007, an effort was made to live-trap both brook trout and char from Big Reed, to hold them in protection at a hatchery, and to spawn them in order to produce pure genetic offspring for restocking in the pond.

The project was fraught with unbelievable difficulties. That year, only one female char and two males were captured. Live-trapping is conducted in the fall, known for unpredictable weather. Due to lack of air transport because of weather, one of these char had to be hand-transported in a cooler over a trail. Mated with the two males, only two of this female's eggs survived. Subsequent matings also experienced high mortality percentages—evidence of the fragility and vulnerability of the char.

As if this weren't enough, it was found that the char kept in a hatchery for future stocking were so "wild" they wouldn't eat the fish food provided for other hatchery trout. They at first would consume only earthworms. Later, they were fooled into eating the nutritious fish pellets by injecting them inside frozen minnows. Finally, they began to thrive on their new diet.

Because of the remoteness of Big Reed, seaplanes and helicopters were the only feasible means of ferrying personnel, equipment, and supplies in and out of the region. Sikorsky, who owns and operates the Bradford Camps, a resort on Munsungan Lake, flies guests in and out by means of a Cessna 172 Skyhawk seaplane.

Though nearly fifty miles from the nearest town, Munsungan is about three air miles from Big Reed Pond. Bradford Camp's guests have fished Big Reed's trout for many decades, hiking in or arriving by floatplane. The pond was so popular with Bradford guests that it built two outlying cabins there during its heyday in the 1950s.

Big Reed had been a "trout factory" in the past, Sikorsky said, and he is confident the reclamation effort will return it to its previous status. He has worked tirelessly to make it happen.

"I have flown for the project officially since 2007—close to a hundred round-trips to Big Reed Pond. That constitutes over $10,000 worth of flying which I have donated to the cause of the project. Some of the flying is to get personnel in and out of Reed, and some for equipment. My last flight out was October 5, 2011, when I flew all the gear out, plus personnel, in ten flights. The project has required a lot of contortionist, back-breaking work in loading and unloading engines, pumps, nets, 35-gallon barrels of chemicals, and numerous external loads of traps, canoes, and lumber."

Sikorsky's upgraded 1968 Cessna Skyhawk is equal to the task of navigating the tight confines of ninety-acre Big Reed. While he has in effect a three-mile water "runway" on Munsungan, Big Reed is about 3,500 feet long, at an elevation slightly over 1,100 median sea level. "I rarely fly out at gross, unless I am blessed with a west wind. But I am regularly out of there with 800 pounds useful, off the water well before halfway, with lots of air below me when I reach the far end."When I'm flying around these wondrous North Maine Woods, I feel very close to my grandfather," Sikorsky continued. "As a young aviator in Russia [before the Revolution], he took off from fields, not airports, and flew without the need for radios and nav aids.

"That is about what it's like for a backcountry float pilot like myself. Every landing has a unique approach, a unique runway, and the flight planning, pilotage, and navigation are particular to each short, local flight that I perform. I have the benefit of more reliable equipment than he had, for certain, but I think the satisfaction and true joy is very much the same."

⟞⟝

While Sikorsky handled the daily flying, two Maine Army National Guard helicopters (appropriately, they were Sikorsky Blackhawks!) hauled the 11,400 pounds of special chemicals required to reclaim the pond.

Project leader Frank Frost said it took eight chopper loads to fly in the chemicals, which were in crates and slung under the helicopters in rope slings. A crew unloaded the slings on the platform. There was only one hitch: On the last load the sling failed to release, and the freight had to be returned to the loading zone. Sikorsky had to fly it in piecemeal.

After applying the chemical treatment to Big Reed, the pond cleansed itself over the next few months. The piscicide rotenone (a natural temporary toxin derived from a South American tree and affecting only gill-breathers) acts by restricting oxygen at the cellular level of the fish. After doing its work, it has a short half-life and becomes ineffective. In fact, not all the trout necessarily die. While chemicals are being pumped into the depths, workers on boats watch for any struggling fish that come to the surface. If caught immediately and placed in freshwater, they can be revived with no harm and flown to a hatchery for future stocking.

Sikorsky and his wife, Karen, spent hours in a canoe-and-kayak "catamaran" he put together with lumber and straps, helping to net and then attempting to revive any trout or char. No char were found, indicative of the sad state of that population. Forty brook trout were netted, thirteen of which were successfully revived in freshwater. They were placed in a special tank that contained an oxygen system, and flown by Igor to a fish culture station (hatchery).

Application of the rotenone was similar to a military operation. Director of IF&W's fisheries division, Peter Bourque, said it involved biologists and their support staffs from all of Maine's fisheries regions, plus several volunteers—some twenty-five in all. Virtually all equipment and supplies—including boats, pumps, and the crews themselves—had to be flown into and out of the small, ninety-acre pond by light floatplane.

There were only two small, primitive fishermen's cabins at Big Reed. Most of the personnel had to be housed some distance away and flown in and out daily. Exacerbating the situation was the fact that all of this took place in the fall, when adverse weather is a constant threat in northern Maine. Sikorsky anticipates many more hours of flight time in order to survey results and monitor environmental effects.

The effort to "reclaim" Big Reed was intense, rigorous, logistically nightmarish, and very costly for the Maine Department of Inland Fisheries and Wildlife, already under financial constraints. It continues to seek funding assistance from outside sources for the project. According to fisheries director Peter Bourque (now retired), the total cost "will be very scary."

The fee for chemicals alone was some $36,000. Another $75,000 was contracted to a private hatchery for "culturing" the fish; that is, spawning them and raising the young trout. Add in all the other expenses—personnel, transportation, restocking, environmental monitoring, etc.—and the total will not be known for years. Bourque said the funds came primarily from the IF&W's general budget (25 percent) and the Federal Aid in Sport Fish Restoration Act (75 percent). The Department also received a contribution from The Nature Conservancy, and "lots of free camp rental and aircraft time from Bradford Camps and other private contributions from Igor's clientele."

Sikorsky estimates his business donated over $20,000 in flying and cabin services. But he gained a fair amount of satisfaction from the project: "I had the duty, honor, and privilege of flying these fish from Reed to their sanctuary—in Gary Picard's private hatchery, Mountain Springs Trout Farm," he said.

Frost recalls, "It was certainly a grind, and I underestimated just how hard it would be, and how much work it would take to get it done. The key to our success in such a remote location was the availability of aircraft: Igor's 172, our own Warden Service 185s, and the National Guard's Blackhawks."

Sikorsky adds, "Final success will be when we see the tiny char fry in the pond, showing that they are truly wild again." Even though Big Reed Pond is restricted to catch-and-release and fly-fishing only, he says they are not encouraging any fishing for a year or two. Several years should allow the fish to become well reestablished. Strict regulations will hopefully prevent another illegal stocking of exotic and harmful fish.

Was all of this worth it, to save one small, isolated pond and its unique populations of trout? Frost and the committee of interested professionals and lay supporters with which he worked think it was.

"I think we caught it just in time," he said.

Update:

In 2012 the Big Reed Pond was restocked with 99 arctic char and 3,186 brook trout. All of these fish came from matings of the original trout and char that had been removed prior to the treatment of the pond with piscicide.

Frost's staff, with the assistance of University of Maine researchers, continues to monitor and analyze the progress of recovery, including the movement of the tagged char. "We have determined that six of the ten acoustic-tagged char are still alive."

In the fall of 2012, biologists live-trapped 19 char and 428 brook trout, ranging from 4.3 to 13.7 inches. "Since char mature and reproduce at older ages than brook trout, determination of a successfully spawning population will likely be later," Frost said.

Fortunately, no rainbow smelts—the illegally introduced species that decimated the habitat for trout and char, and were the primary target of the reclamation effort—were found.

"The brook trout released at Big Reed Pond and its tributaries in 2011 and 2012 have survived well and exhibited good growth. The likelihood of restoring trout in the near future is very high," Frost said.

Sikorsky reported: "The project is gravely in need of money to finance the final two years of hatchery growing and rearing expenses. The state has tapped all the resources it can at this point. The Nature Conservancy has agreed to receive money earmarked for the project, with 100 percent of the donations going directly to the hatchery contract."

Donations, which are tax-exempt (write "Reed Pond Project" on check), may be sent to The Nature Conservancy, 14 Maine Street, Suite 401, Brunswick, Maine 04011.

A version of this story appeared in Aircraft
Owners and Pilots Association's (AOPA) *PILOT*
magazine (March 2011).

14

It's Raining Trout

Flyovers Replenish Maine's Fish Stocks

MY WIFE LORRAINE AND I were enjoying a quiet day of fishing on a remote Maine trout pond one fall when my ears perked up at the sound of a light plane. As an old ex-pilot, I of course couldn't resist craning around for a look. I turned just in time to see a low flying Cessna floatplane approaching. At that instant, a gush of foaming water blossomed out and streamed back from each side of the pontoons, and several hundred slim, dark shapes came arcing down and splashed into the pond a couple hundred feet from our canoe, as the pilot throttled up and roared away overhead.

Our small pond was receiving its annual stocking of brook trout—in spectacular fashion.

The technique of stocking fish by dropping them from the air was developed by Maine Warden Service air crews. Maine has hundreds of small ponds, many located in remote areas and inaccessible by roads. Many are popular with anglers, who may reach them by hiking—or, if the pond is large enough—flying in by bush planes. This increasing popularity and pressure mean that existing native fish populations often must be supplemented by stocking.

As early as the 1940s and '50s, Maine warden pilots began stocking ponds from the air. Initially, an old Stinson Reliant was equipped with interior tanks, with chutes opening through the bottom of the fuselage. The pilot released the fish by reaching back and pulling hand levers. Later, as wardens began flying more modern Super Cubs and Cessnas, they designed and perfected the current system of pontoon-mounted tanks.

Presently, the warden fleet comprises three Cessna 185s mounted on floats in the summer and wheel-skis during the winter months.

The torpedo-shaped plastic tanks, mounted on each pontoon, are designed so they are held upright by a heavy pin in a slot at the front. They are off balance, so when the pin is retracted by a solenoid controlled by a switch in the cockpit, the tanks tip outward, dumping the fish and water. They are individually controlled, so the pilot can select to drop either tank, or both simultaneously. Each tank is equipped with an oxygen system, controlled from the cockpit, to keep the water well oxygenated and the fish lively and healthy during the flight from stocking truck to pond.

Each tank holds twenty-five to thirty gallons of water and ninety pounds of trout. In the case of legal-size trout (eight to twelve inches long), anywhere from 300 to 350 trout occupy each tank.

Annually, the Maine warden pilots stock approximately a quarter-million fish (mainly brook trout, but also some land-locked salmon and splake, a hybrid of brook and lake trout) in 150 to 160 ponds in areas inaccessible to trucks. This is roughly 15 to 20 percent of the 1.5 million or so stocked each year, according to hatcheries superintendent Steve Wilson.

The normal drill is that one or more tank trucks are loaded with thousands of fish at one of the Department hatcheries early in the morning, and driven to a rendezvous point at a lake. The three planes—often supplemented by a Cessna 185 and pilot loaned from the Maine Department of Conservation, in order to expedite the process—land at the lake and taxi to the shore, where a ground crew awaits. The crew members fill the seaplanes' fish tanks with freshwater from the lake and then dump in the squirming trout, which have been carefully weighed and counted. The pilots receive instructions as to the locations of ponds and quantities of fish each pond is to receive.

And then comes the takeoff and flight—sometimes exciting, because the load of heavy water and aeration equipment can come close to the aircraft's gross payload.

Aerial stocking occurs in the spring and fall, with the bulk of the drops made in late September to early October. This is close to the end of the fishing season. The trout then have all winter to become acquainted with their new "home," and become acclimated to the wild and to foraging on their own before the next fishing season rolls around. The fall stocking usually coincides with the peak of the foliage season.

During the years I worked at Inland Fisheries and Wildlife I frequently flew with the warden pilots on stocking flights.

As the plane lifts from the water, there is that thrill of flight. The shoreside trees dip below the nose and pass underneath. The world opens around you—a world of vast forests, blue lakes dotted with toy-like boats, and distant blue mountains. The leaves are turning color and the hillsides form a tapestry of orange and gold and scarlet. In the intensity of takeoff, you've forgotten all about the "passengers" sharing this plane ride.

Then you glance down through the plane's side window at the large, red, rocket-shaped tank fastened to the top of the pontoon. The wind blast from the slipstream lashes the surface of the water in the tank, mixing a good supply of oxygen into the water. Under the ruffled surface you can make out the dim forms of swimming fish. They swim agilely about the tank, unaware that they are now being flown a thousand feet above the ground, and unknowing that in a few minutes they will face the most exciting adventure of their lives.

As the plane approaches the designated pond, the pilot throttles back and sets up his approach by adjusting engine power and flaps for a gradual descent. Ideal drop speed is approximately 70 knots, and at treetop level (fifty to seventy feet above ground level). This dissipates the forward motion of the fish and ensures that they will fall straight down to penetrate the water, rather than skipping along the surface, in order to minimize the shock.

The trout hit the water with a splash. Instantly, they dive and disappear.

This method doesn't traumatize the fish. Department biologists using scuba gear have had trout dropped around them and observed the fish as they hit the water and swam away. The biologists report that most of the trout easily survive their aerial drop without injury or harm.

The warden pilots have racked up a remarkable record of success and safety over the decades, while hauling millions of fish on thousands of fish-dropping missions. Often, this is flying under tough conditions. Many of the smaller ponds are tucked up in the mountains—sometimes almost surrounded by granite peaks. Pilots must sometimes thread their way up narrow, twisting valleys, dodging tall trees and craggy cliffs. Then there's always the weather to contend with—mountain squalls, scud, gusty winds while delicately maneuvering a heavily loaded and aerodynamically "dirty" aircraft at low airspeed.

⋙⋘

There have been some misses and mishaps.

One pilot of my acquaintance once found himself in a fuel-starved situation while engrossed in a long, tiring day and was forced to land in a rough clearing. The floats were damaged but the plane and pilot survived to fly again. Another pilot, landing in rough conditions on Rangeley Lake, had his plane hit by a powerful wind gust which forced the floats under and flipped the plane over onto its back. He was rescued by a passing boater, and the aircraft was subsequently hauled ashore and restored to airworthy condition. And there have been a few "misses," when fish inadvertently have dropped on land instead of hitting the water. This usually occurs at the smallest, trickiest ponds in the mountains, when unpredictable wind gusts can blow the falling fish off course.

A pilot had a problem one day at a tiny pond in eastern Maine, when one of his tanks delayed tripping when he flipped the switch. A couple of fishermen, approaching the pond through the woods, heard a plane roar overhead, and seconds later trout began falling down through the tree branches around them, flopping at their feet. The pair failed to make the connection between plane and fish. Later that day when they encountered a crew stocking fish in a brook, they approached the men and said: "You guys ain't gonna believe this, but . . ."

⋙⋘

Brook trout are among nature's most beautiful and admired creatures. They provide beauty and pleasure (and excellent eating) to many. But trout are extremely vulnerable. They can't tolerate competition for food and space from more-aggressive fish species. They do best when they alone occupy a body of water. They can live only in water that is very pure and cold. They cannot survive in warmer, dirty waters. Also, trout are slow to reproduce themselves, so even where the environmental conditions are good, their numbers are rapidly depleted by heavy fishing pressure. Even at best, trout are very short-lived. A three-year-old trout is old; few trout live to the age of four or five years.

All of which adds up to the need for stocking these waters. In order to provide trout fishing for today's anglers, biologists have had to resort to artificial methods to increase trout reproduction. Thus, the need for hatcheries and stocking programs— even in remote, small Maine ponds where stocking by air is the only feasible and cost-effective method.

Aerial stocking of trout is exciting and colorful. It's also less expensive and faster than stocking by truck or backpack. It makes possible the stocking of remote ponds that could not be reached any other way. Best of all, it assures that trout fishing remains available to many present-day anglers who would otherwise be deprived of the pleasure of seeing, and fishing for, these beautiful rare gems of nature.

This story first appeared in the May 2006 issue
of Aircraft Owners and Pilots Association's
(AOPA) *PILOT* magazine.

Part 3:
On Wing

15

One Bird at a Time

The Battle to Save Maine's Bald Eagles

IN A SYMPHONY OF GRACEFUL MOTION, the big white seagull swooped and soared in the unseen power of the cold northwest wind. A dozen times it glided down toward the wooden feeding station, but each time veered off nervously at the last moment.

Finally, gingerly, the gull settled in for a landing. The winter sun shone brilliantly from a brittle January sky. Through the long lens of my camera the gull appeared only a few feet away. I could clearly see its red eye flicking nervously about, the chill wind rippling the feathers on its neck.

Arrayed at its feet on the feeding station was a smorgasbord of seagull delights: chunks of suet, fish, and red meat. All frozen solid. And cut, by design, to a size impossible for even a gluttonous gull to swallow intact.

The gull poked among the food in hopes of finding a piece small enough to swallow whole. It gulped down a couple of tidbits—enough to whet its appetite. After swiveling its head nervously, scanning the skies, the gull snatched a hard chunk of suet in its beak and took wing. The bird's flight was erratic and clumsy as it struggled with the heavy load, intent on carrying it off to a quiet place to be picked apart and eaten.

Observing this little drama beside me was an apparition-like figure in a wheelchair: Bob Hawkes, wearing dark clothes and a black hood with eyehole cutouts and holding a movie camera in black-gloved hands.

Suddenly, Bob, who had been watching from the shadows, pushed his wheelchair close to the window, grabbed up the old Bolex camera on his lap, and began shooting film.

Then I, too, saw what Bob's sharp eyes had already spotted. A large, mature bald eagle, its white head and tail gleaming in the bright sun, was flying toward us from its perch tree a quarter-mile away across Maine's Penobscot River.

The gull, flying out over the river, had seen the eagle, too. Its wings beat frantically as it flared and attempted to turn back toward the shore and the safety of the trees. But even a seagull is no match for the swift, menacing flight of a hungry eagle. Preferring to give up its food to the risk of itself becoming the eagle's dinner, the gull released the chunk of suet and swerved off upriver, squalling in anger and fright.

The eagle folded its wings and plummeted like a comet after the falling suet. It flared out and snatched the chunk just as it hit the water. Then it flew off to dine at leisure on its favorite perch tree.

══▓╞⓾╝▓══

Bob Hawkes witnessed many a similar "mugging" from his observation post at the picture window of his home in Orrington, Maine.

While most bird feeders are stocked with sunflower seeds for chickadees and nuthatches (the Hawkes also had several of these out), Bob's feeding station held big chunks of deer meat, cut-up chickens with feathers and entrails intact, pieces of fish and beef suet, and occasionally even parts of road- or dog-killed deer.

Its most frequent—and noisy—patrons were seagulls. But the feeding station's real purpose was to attract Bob's most welcome visitors: remnants of the dwindling New England bald eagle population that wintered along these tidal water stretches of the lower Penobscot River.

Bob Hawkes, then in his fifties, was paraplegic. He had been wheelchair-bound since a spinal injury. When I asked Bob about it, he modestly passed it off as a "haying accident." Later an acquaintance of his told me that Bob had been helping a friend get his crop of hay into a barn. Suddenly Bob saw a heavy lift, used for raising the hay, tear loose from its support and begin falling toward a hay wagon under which several children were lying in the shade, watching the haying operation. Bob, in a herculean effort, managed to break the fall of the heavy machinery and hold it long enough for the youngsters to scramble to safety. But the weight crushed his back, paralyzing him for life.

Bob earned his living as a speech and hearing specialist, working with handicapped children in Maine schools. He was actively involved in wheelchair athletic programs such as swimming and basketball, and won several state championships. And his driving energy and enthusiasm served to inspire the teachers and students with whom he worked.

After his work, one of the consuming interests in Bob's life was the eagles that wintered on the tidal portion of the Penobscot River below Bangor.

The Hawkes home sat on a high rocky ledge, which Bob and his wife Becky whimsically called Peregrine Bluff. It overlooked a wild stretch of the river where ice sheets drift up- and

downstream with the tides, and eagles soar the winds rising
from the ledgy riverbanks, searching for food. And therein was
one of their greatest threats to survival.

⧫×⧫

Eagles, which feed at the top of the food chain, had been
harmed by the immense quantities of hard pesticides such as
DDT that humans had for decades been applying to the land.
These inevitably washed down brooks and streams into the
rivers, lakes, and ocean. And even though these harsh pesticides
have been banned in this country for several years, they persist
in the environment and will remain with us for many years, perhaps centuries. An added menace is the closely related PCBs.

At all stages, from the tiniest planktonic life up the chain,
water-living organisms ingest and concentrate these poisons,
passing them on up to the next predator that devours them.
The eagle gets it all.

From the 1950s to the 1970s, known bald eagle nestings
in some parts of Maine failed to produce young. The cause?
Excessive amounts of pesticide residues stored in their bodies,
causing the eagles to lay sterile, thin-shelled eggs. These eggs
failed to hatch and were eventually abandoned by the parents
to rot in the nest.

The US Fish and Wildlife Service Research Station at Patux-
ent, Maryland, analyzed two such eggs removed from separate
nests on the Kennebec River. The scientist in charge, Dr. Stanley Wiemeyer, reported that they contained the highest levels
of DDT and PCBs ever analyzed in eagle eggs. The shells were
30 percent thinner than normal.

The root of the eagles' reproductive failure lay in their
food source. Eagles are primarily fish eaters. Whereas they

Bald eagle carries a stick in its claws to build a new nest.

occasionally feed upon carrion, such as carcasses found in the woods, their nests are normally constructed near water, and they depend upon fish as their main food. Unfortunately, fish were also the prime source of hydrocarbon residues which proved deadly to eagles.

During a summer of observing a nesting pair at Merrymeeting Bay, I saw the eagles carrying only eels to the nest for food. These were abundant in the then heavily polluted waters.

A University of Maine biologist, Dr. Ray "Bucky" Owen, said that on the basis of many observations, eagles wintering on the Penobscot River near Bangor subsisted almost entirely upon eels and mergansers, fish-eating ducks that winter in great numbers in the open, tidal portions of the river.

The eagles perched on trees on the riverbank near flocks of feeding ducks. When a duck surfaced with a large eel that it had difficulty swallowing, the eagles would swoop down upon the duck, causing it to drop the eel and dive underwater to evade the eagle's deadly talons. The eagle then snatched up the eel and flew off to a favorite perch to feed. Occasionally, the eagles picked off a merganser that failed to submerge in time. Since the mergansers' bodies were also loaded with toxic residues, the result was the same.

I witnessed an illustration of this one bitter cold winter, sitting with Bob and Becky Hawkes in their cozy living room. As we watched, an immature eagle flew out from its perch across the river and began harassing a small bunch of feeding mergansers. Suddenly the eagle swooped down and stole an eel literally from a duck's mouth. Then, as the young eagle tried to fly off, it dropped its prize into the water. But the eaglet folded its six-foot wings and followed the eel down, plunging right underwater after it.

Whether it was the clumsy act of a youngster or a deliberate dive, we couldn't say, but it was the first time any of us had ever witnessed such a midwinter dunking in ice-clogged waters.

The eagle surfaced with the eel in its beak. Then, awkwardly using its wings as paddles, it flopped and "rowed" its way to a large nearby ice floe and clumsily climbed out. Another eagle, drawn by the commotion, flew down and landed nearby. The wet eagle ignored the visitor. It shook itself a bit and proceeded to calmly feast on its eel.

Apparently a midwinter dunking in near-zero weather was considerably less threatening to a hungry eagle than were the lethal poisons contained in the food they innocently ingested.

In the hope of enticing eagles from contaminated foods, attempts were made to provide the birds with "clean" sustenance—attempts based upon the success of Bob Hawkes's feeding station.

With the help of some of his biology students at the university, Owen constructed several feeding platforms patterned

photo from Anita and Paul Fournier collection; courtesy of Maine State Museum

Pair of eagles at their nest. Male is settling down on female's back to mate.

closely after the one built by Hawkes. These were placed at spots along the river where eagles were known to perch and feed. They were liberally supplied with chunks of red meat from moose and deer killed in collisions with vehicles on the highways or confiscated from poachers.

The eagles shunned the new feeders. During countless hours of observation, no eagle was seen to visit a feeder, let alone take any of its food.

The birds totally ignored a similar feeding station set up by federal and state wildlife officials at a game preserve in Merrymeeting Bay on the Kennebec River.

Meanwhile, eagles perched in the trees in Bob and Becky Hawkeses' yard, harassing and robbing gulls, and occasionally dropping down to snatch up a morsel themselves.

The reason? Bob and Becky had had their feeding station there for nearly ten years. It took five years before they ever saw an eagle actually come to the feeder. The wary eagles took that long to accept the feeding platform as safe. In fact, Bob eventually removed the platform and presented his meat offerings on the ground. Eagles are suspicious of man-made structures and prefer their food as they normally find it in the wild.

Following several unsuccessful seasons in which no eagles could be enticed to artificially placed food, the government and university teams dropped their efforts at winter feeding. Only the Hawkeses' program was a continued success.

Then the couple began to experience problems with locating food sources. In the 1970s, the University of Maine, in cooperation with the Department of Inland Fisheries and Wildlife, became heavily involved in research work on the northeastern coyote invasion of Maine. Most of the available meat from deer and moose carcasses was used for feeding coyotes, whose behavior was being studied. There was no longer a surplus for eagles.

Bob and Becky made regular visits to meat and food stores in the Bangor area, buying suet and meat scraps for gulls and eagles with money from their own pockets.

The population of the bald eagle, the symbol of our nation, remained in a precarious and threatened situation. Where once tens of thousands of eagles thrived, only a few thousand breeding pairs remained. Man's progress was destroying their habitat, polluting the waters, and poisoning the eagles' (and our own) sources of food.

But on cold winter mornings, after Becky Hawkes had trudged through the dawn snow to replenish the feeding platform, some of these young eagles joined their elders perching in the trees of Peregrine Bluff, and learned to swoop down and steal their breakfast from the scavenging gulls.

Thus kept away from a full diet of poisonous fish and ducks, these young eagles lived long enough to allow the environment to slowly cleanse itself of man's poisonous effluents and added their own progeny to the Maine skies.

Author's note: *When the original magazine article was written in the mid-1970s, Maine had the only remaining bald eagles on the entire Eastern Seaboard, north of Chesapeake Bay. Maine's population at the time was down to about thirty nests, and most were not producing young. This was true throughout most of the Lower Forty-Eight. The culprit was the widespread spraying of insecticides, including DDT, on crops and timberlands. The eagles, predators at the top of the food chain, ingested these pesticides in the food they ate—primarily fish, but also fish-eating ducks that were also loaded with the poisons.*

Birds of a Feather

The eggs laid by the eagles were infertile and often thin-shelled, and never hatched. Two eagle eggs retrieved from nests on the lower Kennebec River contained the highest levels of DDT residues ever analyzed in eagle eggs.

The type of feeding program pioneered by Bob Hawkes was aimed at providing eagles wintering in Maine with meat free of pesticides. It took many years, but the United States Fish and Wildlife Service, the University of Maine, and the Department of Inland Fisheries and Wildlife later used winter feeding programs patterned on the Hawkeses' efforts to conduct extensive eagle feeding programs along the Maine coast, using road-killed deer and moose and furbearer carcasses provided by trappers.

The courageous man portrayed in this story, Robert Hawkes, retired to Florida shortly after this article was published, and the author has long since lost contact with him. He was in his fifties some thirty years ago.

After DDT use was banned in the 1970s, bald eagles in Maine and other parts of the country began a gradual but remarkable increase. According to wildlife biologist Charles Todd of the Maine Department of Inland Fisheries and Wildlife, who has been working with Maine eagles for over a quarter-century, the current Maine bald eagle population stands at over a thousand, with about 450 active nests.

An earlier version of this story appeared in *The Country Gentleman* (Autumn 1976).

16

Silent Ghost of the North

The Great Gray Owl

THE HUGE GRAY BIRD with its strangely piercing yellow eyes and incongruous white mustache sat eerily silent on its high perch in a wind-blasted maple tree. The below-zero wind tearing through this woods in central Maine lashed its long, ragged, gray, white-streaked feathers, which appeared to be only loosely attached to its body.

The bird paid no attention to me. I was hunched in my thick parka and partially hidden by brush, more to avoid the chilling blasts than for concealment. But its eyes were sharp and focused on a spot in the snow at the edge of a clearing, where a field mouse had just emerged and was scampering about in the dazzlingly bright winter sun. I kept my eye glued to the viewfinder of my camera, and followed the bird as it launched from its perch.

It dove almost straight down, gaining flight speed, and leveled off just a few feet above the ground, flapping and gliding as it swiftly, silently, zeroed in on its prey. At the last instant, its feet tucked up under its chin and it struck—and missed with its grasping talons.

It was the only such miss I observed in a number of mouse captures over a period of several days. But the mouse had been

photo from Anita and Paul Fournier collection; courtesy of Maine State Museum
Approaching prey, a great gray owl keeps its eyes fixed on the rodent.

hit and dazed. In a maneuver surprisingly adroit and swift in so large a bird, it immediately swept around and pounced again. This time it grasped the mouse in its talons.

Then, as I'd seen it do a number of times, the bird simply sat on the snow, holding the mouse in its death grip while seeming to casually look around. Finally it reached down and snatched the mouse in its beak by the back of the neck and flew back up to its tree perch. After sitting there for several minutes, again coolly scanning the scene, it began swallowing the mouse whole—head first, in several gulps. The tail hung outside the beak for a moment before it, too, disappeared down the hatch.

To most of us, the great gray owl is the eeriest, least known of birds. Few, outside of researchers, have ever seen this rarest of northern predators, though it is one of the world's biggest. On those rare occasions when it *is* observed, it usually sits immobile on a tree or post.

Strix nebulosa presents an awesome, spooky appearance to those relatively few who have been privileged to observe it. That is partly due to its quietness. It is one of the most silent of large birds, its low-pitched hoot heard only occasionally, and mainly during the breeding period in late winter.

Its flight is mysteriously noiseless, too. Thick, soft feathers conceal any sound from the beating wings. The bird's aura of mystery is also due to its apparent size. At twenty-four to thirty-three inches tall when perched, and with a five-foot wingspread, it is the most impressive owl. The size is a bit deceiving, however. Under that great mass of loose feathers and down, evolved to protect it from the cold climate where it lives, the actual size of the great gray owl is slightly smaller than the snowy owl.

Winter migration for most birds means flying to the warm and sunny Southland. But for some great gray owls in some winters, a vacation "south" means the snowy and frigid countryside of several northern border states, including Maine. Not considered true migrants, great grays will move from their nesting territories in search of food when it fails locally. When they do move into more southerly regions than normal, they usually do so in numbers—a phenomenon called an "irruption." These large owls normally live in the subarctic regions of Canada, Alaska, and in several northwestern states, especially in the higher altitudes of the Sierras and Rockies, as well as in parts of northern Europe including Scandinavia, Russia, and Asia. Some are known to nest as far east as Minnesota and Michigan. Living secretly in thick evergreen forests, they are rarely seen.

In some years, a failure of the mast crop (seeds and nuts) up north results in a crash in the populations of small rodents such as lemmings, field mice, voles, and the like, which normally make up the owls' diet. This shortage can send the great grays south and east of their normal range in search of prey. Since these giant owls come from the northern latitudes where in summertime there is little or no darkness, they are not strictly nocturnal hunters but frequently forage in the daytime.

⸏⸎

I observed the pair of owls pictured in this chapter during the month of February. They spent a few weeks catching mice and other small rodents in a farming region of central Maine. I had been alerted to their presence by an old acquaintance, Frank Gramlich, who at the time (prior to his retirement) was the US Fish and Wildlife agent for the state of Maine. "These birds showed up here because they've been starving up north where they normally live," Frank told me.

I asked his permission before approaching to photograph the owls so I would not disturb them or disrupt their normal lives. Frank assured me that as long as I remained quiet and made no sudden or threatening moves, they should tolerate my presence. "These owls live far away from humans, and have developed little fear of us. You should be okay."

He was right. The owls paid little or no attention to me as long as I kept a comfortable distance. This provided an incredible opportunity to observe these unique birds and their foraging technique for many cold but fascinating hours. Temperatures averaged zero degrees Fahrenheit or lower, with bitter winds.

Burrs are stuck to tail feathers of a perched owl.

I saw the owls daily, flying and foraging in full daylight. They had selected as their winter territory a farm area dominated by a large chicken barn with a grain silo, which attracted many rodents.

The great gray, like the snowy owl, is remarkably well adapted to survive in the harsh northern winters. It's covered with a coat of brownish-gray feathers, under which is a thick insulating layer of down. Even its legs and feet down to their toenails are covered with down and feathers for protection from the cold.

photo from Anita and Paul Fournier collection; courtesy of Maine State Museum

This head-and-shoulders view of the great gray owl shows its curious white mustache and neat, black "bow tie." The strong, cold wind moves the loose, long feathers on its breast.

The owl has distinctive yellow eyes and a round "Charlie Brown" head with no ear tufts. And it has rather comical white chin whiskers, and a neat, black "bow tie."

The round facial disc and circles of feathers surrounding each eye serve a vital function. They funnel sound to the hidden ear canals, providing the owl with very sensitive hearing. Great grays are able to hear the slight scratching of mice and voles under up to a foot of snow and capture them by plunging down into the snow and snaring them in their claws. I've observed the owls sitting still and quiet on the snow for long periods. I assume they were listening for mice.

Unlike their cousin, the smaller, endangered northern spotted owl (*Strix occidentalis*), the great gray owl is not under special
protections, but is protected by federal and state statutes. While
not considered endangered or threatened because of its large
circumpolar range, the owl depends upon trees for protective
cover and especially for nest sites.

Great grays do not build nests, but take over abandoned nests
of other large birds, such as hawks, crows, and ravens. They also
sometimes nest in the tops and hollows of broken-off tree snags.
They have been known to utilize man-made nesting platforms.
Unfortunately, they sometimes nest atop power-line poles,
which can result in death by electrocution when their long wings
ground the lines. Their preferred nest site is high above the
ground away from predators. Their eggs and young are subject
to predation from hawks, ravens, and another notorious owl, the
great horned, as well as from martens and wolverines.

By depriving them of nesting habitat, heavy timber harvesting
and especially clear cutting are disastrous to great gray owls. Forest fires, on the other hand, can be beneficial, as they leave abundant snags for nest trees, and the regenerating forest can provide
abundant forage in the form of field mice, voles, and such.

Great gray owls have been observed engaged in mating
displays as early as late winter, when snow may still be on the
nest. The male courts his mate by bringing food, which the
pair swaps back and forth. The sexes are indistinguishable by
sight—though, as in some other large predatory birds, including bald eagles, the female may be slightly larger.

Incubation of the clutch of two to five eggs, and in some
cases up to nine, takes twenty-eight to twenty-nine days. The
male does the hunting and provides the family's food. Most
researchers say the female does all of the incubating. Some

say the male shares the incubating to give his mate a break. It's not easy to be certain, since the male and female look so much alike. After the young hatch, the female tears the food into small pieces and feeds it to the young.

Clutch size and survival of the young depend upon the availability of forage and hunting success. When food is abundant, clutches are big, and more young are successfully raised to fledge. In times of scarcity, pairs may not nest at all. In about eight weeks the young fledge, but they may remain near the nest for several months to be fed and cared for.

⊶✕⊷

To most of us, great grays are the antithesis of food. No one, it seems, is interested in partaking of "boiled owl." But that doesn't include some Native Americans of Alaska. According to Tim Osborne of the Alaska Department of Fish and Game, the Athabascan Indians of interior Alaska "consider the bird edible because the owl is fat during the winter. They have named the owl *Nuht-tuhl,* or 'heavy walker.' It is traditional among the Athabascans that only the elders will eat the bird because it is believed if a young person eats it, that person will grow up quickly and die."

Though few of us will ever have the experience of observing a great gray owl, it's comforting to know they are still with us, living out their soundless, enigmatic lives. If we refrain from destroying the last of their habitat or poisoning their prey with our chemicals, perhaps the owls will continue to come south and visit us on occasion, bringing a touch of the northern wild to our world.

17

It Took a Maine Village

How a Couple and Their Neighbors Adopted an Eagle Family

IT WAS ONE OF MID-MAY'S FIRST SOFT EVENINGS in Maine. My wife and I were sitting down to an early supper when the phone rang. The voice on the line was strained and wracked with sobs.

"Someone's just been shooting at the eagles. They're flying around, screaming and having an awful time. I don't know what to do. I don't know if they've shot into the nest and hurt one of the parents, or killed the baby!"

I recognized the voice as that of our friend, Frankie Hatch. She and her husband Duke lived on a Maine lake, and were likely the only couple in the eastern United States whose windows overlooked an active bald eagle's nest. They and their neighbors in the nearby small village of Damariscotta Mills had appointed themselves guardians of the eagle family's welfare.

I calmed Frankie down so she could give me coherent information about this gross act of vandalism.

She had been home alone, watching television, when she was jolted by the crack of a high-powered rifle just outside the house. Startled, she ran outside. Two cars had stopped on the highway and several youths were noisily milling about. One of the young men held a rifle, which he fired again in the direction of the nest.

Frankie, a feisty, sixtyish lady full of fire and vigor, ran down to the edge of the road. "I yelled at them loud as I could. 'What in hell do you think you're doin'?' They all piled into their cars and beat it out of there fast as they could, tires a-squealin'. Only after they were gone did I stop and think: God! They might just as well have taken a shot at me!"

After calming Frankie down again, I called a dispatcher who radioed the nearest game warden and got the forces of the law working on the case. Then I drove the twenty-five-odd miles from my home to hers to look into the situation. We were old acquaintances, but Frankie had called me knowing I'd spent much time observing and filming the nesting eagles as part of my job as an employee of the Maine Department of Inland Fisheries and Wildlife (IF&W).

When I arrived nearly an hour later, serenity had returned to the scene. The sun had just set, and in its afterglow I could see the female's glistening white head above the nest, presumably protecting her young chick hatched only a week ago. Perched watchfully above the nest was the male.

Evidently the shooting incident had been no more than a youthful prank, not an earnest attempt to kill the eagles, which presented an easy target. But the act had been traumatic enough—for the eagles as well as for Frankie Hatch.

(Someone later suggested the youths had shot for the sole purpose of triggering a response from Frankie, whose feistiness was well known in the community. Unfortunately, in her excitement she had not noted any license-plate numbers. The officer had no leads, and the vandals were never caught.)

During the time that these eagles had lived close by Frankie and Duke's mobile home at the foot of Damariscotta Lake (this was during the mid-1970s to '80s), they had experienced a number of such harrowing, even life-threatening incidents. That the eagles survived is due in great part to the protective watchfulness of the Hatches and their neighbors in tiny Damariscotta Mills.

They had reason to be proud and protective. According to the US Fish and Wildlife Service, this was the only known continuously active bald eagle nesting pair during that decade in the eastern United States, between the Penobscot River in Maine and the Chesapeake Bay.

Once there had been tens of thousands of eagles nesting throughout the country, but that was before the introduction of the pesticides DDT and PCB, blamed for rendering bald eagles infertile and decimating their numbers.

Presumably the Damariscotta Lake pair had survived and continued to propagate because the lake and its environs were isolated from polluting factories and intensive agriculture. The lake's fish, the major source of the bald eagles' food, remained relatively free of poisonous chemicals.

It was uncertain just when this pair of eagles had arrived at Damariscotta to take up their territory. Eagles often have two or three nests in close proximity which they alternate using every few years—possibly to escape proliferating parasites in the nest material. Even the local residents were vague as to just when the eagles first arrived. It was thought to be late in the 1960s.

As a wildlife observer and photographer, I began hearing about this elusive pair in the early 1970s. A naturalist friend showed me the location of their first nest, hidden in a thick stand of huge pine trees, in the spring of 1974.

It was a disappointing introduction. The pair had begun nesting earlier in the spring, but then vanished. There were rumors that young boys from the nearby village, enjoying the

sight of the huge, graceful birds in flight, often visited the big
pine nest tree early in the nesting season, and struck at the tree
with sticks to make the birds scream in alarm and fly off. (Ah,
the perpetual peskiness of youth.)

It was feared the eagles wouldn't return. Biologists say eagles
will tolerate very little disturbance around the nest site during
the early stages of incubation. Later, they develop a stronger
attachment or bond to the nest and its eggs and are more likely
to resist disturbance.

In August of that year, I received a surprise call from the
Hatches. The two adult eagles had returned to their territory at
the foot of Damariscotta Lake and were behaving strangely.

Duke, a burly and good-natured retired welder from the
shipyard at Bath, met me in the driveway. We walked to the
edge of the water. He pointed to a tall pine tree on a small
peninsula of land sticking out into the lake, forming a sheltered
cove directly in front of the Hatch home.

"I don't know, but it looks to me like they're trying to build a
new nest in that tree. They've been hauling sticks there yes-
terday and this morning. It's the wrong time of year, but that's
what it looks like they're doing."

As we stood talking I could see the two eagles perched on
separate branches of the pine tree, apparently resting. They
ignored us. Some wildlife observers believe that eagles come to
recognize certain humans whom they see frequently and learn
to trust. This was the case with this pair and the Hatches. The
eagles often flew close to them, and landed in the field behind
their home to pick up grass for the nest, with no apparent fear.
But they steered wide of strangers.

As we talked in plain view of them, one of the eagles
swooped down from its perch and snatched a fish from the

water barely a hundred feet in front of us. I had never seen a wild eagle acting so trustingly near humans before.

In subsequent days, as the eagles continued working on their new nest, I spent as much time as I could in observing and filming them at work.

⟞⟝

To anyone interested in the habits of the huge, graceful bird chosen as the symbol of our nation (over the objections of Benjamin Franklin, who would have preferred the turkey), watching the construction of an eagle's nest is fascinating. The birds work with quiet determination. Each nest requires many thousands of sticks, of many sizes. Both parents work hard at gathering brushwood and bringing it to the nest.

But the female spends much of her time here, choosing and placing sticks with great care until the mix meets with her approval. Sometimes she drops a stick she apparently doesn't like over the side. Often I've seen her tugging and straining to fit in a long, unmanageable limb which her mate had flown in and unceremoniously dumped into the nest—sometimes across her own hardworking back.

I soon came to recognize these two individuals on Damariscotta Lake. Female bald eagles are normally slightly larger than the male. This female had a pure white head. The smaller male had a narrow streak of dark feathers running up the back of his neck to the top of the head.

The sticks bald eagles use in nest-building come from dead trees within about a half-mile radius of the nest. Smaller twigs are obtained by landing on a larger limb and pulling and twisting with the beak until the twig breaks off. Sometimes the eagle

149

lands on the branch it wants, grips it in both feet, and flaps its big wings wildly to break it off.

Most thrilling of all is when the eagle flies full tilt at a large dead limb on a standing tree. At the last moment it cups its wings, brings both clawed feet forward, and smashes into the limb at full flying speed. The eagles seem to be experts at judging the strength of a limb. Usually it snaps off at the trunk and they fly off with it in their claws. A limb seven or eight feet long and two to three inches in diameter is sometimes carried— with difficulty. In a strong wind they really strain hard to gain altitude to reach the high nest. Large sticks are carried in the claws, small twigs in the beak.

Interspersed with stick-carrying flights are claw-fulls of dead grass. This is used to weave in among the sticks to help bind the mass together for stability. The clumps also line the soft "cup" in the center of the finished nest in which the female will lay and incubate her eggs.

One such grass flight nearly ended in tragedy before my eyes. Concealed in a photography blind, I was filming as the male eagle swung to glide into the wind down to a grassy patch between the road and lake. Just then a car was approaching down the road. The eagle swooped just in front of the auto, causing its startled driver to swerve sharply as the six-foot wingspan swept past the windshield.

Unruffled, the eagle lit on the shoulder of the road, grabbed up a double claw-full of grass, and then beat his wings mightily against the stiff wind to carry the grass up to his waiting mate in the nest. I fortunately caught the whole exciting sequence on color movie film.

After spending several weeks of intense activity building their new nest that August, the Damariscotta eagles disappeared.

Their nest-building instinct, possibly heightened by the failed nesting in the spring, had evidently been fulfilled for the season. But they had established a good start on their new home.

⬤━✕━⬤

Between nesting seasons, eagles are believed to range far and wide from their home territories. Their powerful wings and love for soaring high in the winds means they can go up and hitch a ride on a flowing current of air upon which they may be borne hundreds of miles in a few days. They vanish for months. Then they show up again as mating season approaches in late winter.

So it was. On a bright, bitter day in the last week of February I received a call from an excited Frankie Hatch.

"The eagles are back, and are they working hard! They've been hauling sticks to their new nest all morning."

I arrived soon after. Sure enough, something exciting was happening at the south end of Damariscotta Lake. The eagles were working at a frenzied pace.

The entire populace of the nearby small village seemed to take an interest in the eagles and their highly visible nest. Cars and pickup trucks stopped along the lakeside road as their occu-pants watched the birds through binoculars. The eagles, intent on their work, paid them scant attention. The noise of heavy logging and gravel trucks passing by disturbed them not at all.

A local trapper donated several carcasses of skinned-out beavers and otters, which were placed on the ice near the nest. Soon the eagles began coming down from their labors several times a day to feed on the frozen meat.

My wife and I took turns using Duke's ice-fishing hut— barely large enough to accommodate one person at a time—as a photography blind. After the first few days of frantic activity,

151

the eagles slowed their building pace. The nest was ready. For hours on end they roosted and rested in trees. This meant many long, freezing hours in the blind for us. Here Anita's patience was much greater than mine.

I spent one particularly exasperating and long day in the hut. It was bitter cold with a strong wind blowing through the open shooting window. Somewhere just beyond my sight in the trees I could hear the eagles. Occasionally they would send out screeching calls—different vocalizations from their normal ones, with which I had become familiar.

I suspected what they were doing. Late in the afternoon, as the sun was going down and the light beginning to fade, the pair flew into the nest. I decided to stick around a little longer.

A recent thaw followed by a sharp cold snap had turned the frozen lake surface into a smooth sheet of solid ice. Now, just after school and before suppertime, several youngsters from the village appeared, skating on this miles-long rink. Naturally, they gravitated toward the nest, craning their necks to look up at the two birds, which paid them no heed. Two little girls skated up between me and the nest, chattering busily. Then they skated away. The light was marginal for photography. The sun had sunk out of sight.

Suddenly the female let out a hoarse squawk. She flew to a large limb near the top of a dead tree. She called again. Then the male launched into the air. He flew to her, and settled down upon her back. They mated. The male's head was thrown back, his beak wide open, and he screeched his exaltation to the wind and sky as he transferred his life-giving sperm to her.

It was a brief, if joyous, encounter. In a moment he spread his wings, was lifted from his mate's back by the wind, and settled on a nearby limb, where he preened and groomed his

Female adult bald eagle on nest incubating eggs at Damariscotta Lake nest.

feathers. And there they remained, as the darkness settled in and I returned home.

I caught this sequence on film. It appeared on the CBS-TV newsmagazine, *Sunday Morning with Charles Kuralt.*

⚭

In early April a change occurred at the nest. The female settled in for the long incubation period. The male mostly roosted, on guard in a nearby tree. Occasionally he brought a fish—usually it appeared to be an eel—to the nest. Once I saw him fly in with a long snake dangling from his talons. Now and then he took the female's place while she flew off—to feed, or simply to stretch her wings and get some exercise. But mostly she occupied the nest, her white head glistening above the edge.

She remained thus for weeks—through drizzling rainstorms, snow squalls, bitter-cold days, and unseasonably hot spring days. Protected underneath her, the single egg remained at a nearly constant 97 degrees Fahrenheit as its embryo developed—likely the only developing bald eagle egg along a thousand miles of Atlantic coastline.

Around the first of May her behavior changed. No longer was she simply sitting and brooding in the position called "incubation posture" by ornithologists. Now she was more active, lowering her head frequently into the nest, tearing off small bits of food, and spending much of her time in a semi-crouched protective stance. Obviously, the egg had hatched. The male was kept busier than ever, flying out to find food, to supply not only his mate but another hungry mouth with fish.

It was several more agonizing weeks before the youngster was old and big enough to provide us our first glimpse of itself—a round, grayish, huge-beaked blob of down staggering clumsily and comically about the nest. One or both doting parents were constantly in the nest, protecting and caring for the helpless youngster.

It's amazing how rapidly an eaglet grows and develops on the protein-rich fish diet supplied by its parents. By the time the chick was six weeks old it weighed several pounds and was shedding its down coat in favor of a growing mass of gray-brown feathers.

At this point a crew under the direction of Francis Gramlich, Maine-based biologist for the US Fish and Wildlife Service, arrived to band the eaglet. An experienced biologist climbed the tall pine tree, captured the wildly flailing youngster by its legs, flopped it onto its back, and affixed a numbered metal tag to one leg. Meanwhile, the parents, screaming defiance, swooped and circled the nest. They approached menacingly close, but never quite struck the climber.

The final month of an eaglet's life in the nest is one of apparent solitude. The parents are seldom there, except briefly to drop off fish. But they are always close at hand, roosting in nearby trees. No activity near the nest escapes their notice. Any perceived threat to the nest launches the pair, circling and screaming in alarm.

The youngster, between periods of feeding and dozing, progressively becomes more active. As its wings grow to their incredible span, the eaglet spends much of its time flapping and exercising them, gaining power and control over these huge six-foot airfoils. It hops up and down several inches above the nest, flapping furiously for minutes at a time, before flopping back down into the nest to rest.

Then, in late July, our eaglet fledged. One minute it was in the nest, stretching its wings. The next instant it was airborne, winging to a nearby tree, with seemingly little effort or clumsiness. It would spend a few weeks in the vicinity of the nest, sometimes sleeping in it, sometimes roosting in a tree. The parents remained nearby, bringing food to the youngster several times a day. But then it was gone. For good.

There are many hazards in the life of a newly fledged eagle. That same fall, two immature eagles were found shot to death in Maine. One was identified as a bird banded that summer in a

photo from Anita and Paul Fournier collection; courtesy of Maine State Museum
First eaglet adopted and raised by Maine eagles at Swan Island from egg transferred from Minnesota, May 1976.

nest in eastern Maine, near Machias. The other's feet had been cut off from the body, and the leg band was missing. It could have been the Damariscotta eaglet.

Frank Gramlich and other eagle biologists suspect that young eagles use their powerful new flight ability to range far, even hundreds of miles, from their home territory during the first few years of their lives before reaching maturity at about the age of five years. Evidence of the wide dispersal (and vulnerability) of young eagles was the discovery of an immature bird from Maine that had become entangled in a fishing net and drowned in South Carolina.

Gramlich, who worked with the Maine eagles for many years, estimated that a high percentage of young eagles fail to reach maturity (when their tail and head feathers turn white, at about four or five years of age). "The modern world is full of hazards to the young eagle," he said.

For instance, in Maine at that time there were some fifty known active nests. With the lone exception of the Damariscotta Lake nest, all were located in a sparsely populated region of eastern Maine, where pollution and pesticides use had been slight. These nests were producing an average of thirty to forty eaglets annually. Yet the population continued to decline, losing one to two nests per year.

"I'm afraid we're losing our breeding birds," Gramlich reported at that time. One long-active nest was destroyed when someone shot and killed one of the adults. Its mate disappeared; the nest remained empty. Another long-established nesting pair near Machias failed to return in the spring after an adult eagle had been sighted in the vicinity with a steel trap and chain dangling from its foot as it awkwardly tried to fly.

For some twenty years the Damariscotta eagles almost miraculously survived the odds against them—and, indeed, continued to produce young each spring since they took up residence. Many seasons they produced two fledglings each year. There's no doubt that one major reason was the dedicated vigilance of Duke and Frankie Hatch and their neighbors in the village.

Not all of the eagles' problems are caused by humans. Some of their fiercest competitors for territorial space and fishing rights are ospreys—large fish hawks. For years there were two active osprey nests within a couple of miles of the Damariscotta eagles, and they made frequent forays. A major attraction for both eagles and ospreys here is the annual run of alewives—small saltwater fish which run up the outlet stream in the hundreds of thousands each spring and provide an easy food supply for the birds just at the right time to coincide with the nesting season.

Eagles have a reputation for stealing fish from ospreys, but on several occasions I saw ospreys dive-bomb the eagles near their nest. Frankie and Duke often saw ospreys attack the nest, apparently bent on killing the young. Duke once observed an eagle and osprey locked in combat above the cove. The eagle finally forced the osprey under the water and flew back to the nest.

"I thought the osprey was done for, but after a while it recovered and flew off," Duke said.

Another woman from the village, who spent much time observing the pair, told me she once saw several ospreys attacking the nest, repeatedly trying to reach and kill the eaglet. The female eagle repelled their charges by lying on her back in the nest, lethal claws slashing in the air whenever they approached. The two eagles finally drove the ospreys away.

Eagles consider the area in front of their nest as their private domain. They permit no other predatory birds near it. They especially seem to abhor great blue herons—big, clumsy, ungainly birds which seem quite harmless. No heron is allowed to fish nearby. When one did sneak into the Damariscotta cove unnoticed one day, the eagles attacked it so furiously that it scuttled into the woods and hid rather than attempting to fly away.

Particularly vexing to this pair of eagles were the ubiquitous, noisome, exploitive seagulls, especially the great blackbacks, which nearly equal the eagles in size and boldness. They are especially numerous in May, when the alewives run up into the lake and provide food for many species of predators.

Seagulls continually tried to pick up fish near the eagles' cove. If they got too close, they were driven off by the eagles, who sometimes forced the gulls to drop their fish and then swooped down and snatched it for themselves.

One spring day I saw the eagles fighting off a large flock of blackbacks. This was in early May, when the chick was still small and helpless. Both eagles left the nest unguarded for a moment, and several gulls swooped down, apparently intent on picking off the fat, succulent baby. But the eagles returned in time, and the gulls, intimidated by the fiercely protective parents, wheeled off noisily down the lake in search of easier prey.

The Damariscotta Mills villagers' interest in the welfare of their eagle family was constant. Any unusual human activity around the nest was swiftly reported to wildlife officials. The people remained vigilant and protective.

One day, an eaglet not quite ready to master its wings blew out of the nest and onto the road in front of a passing vehicle. The occupants, two men unknown to local residents, picked up the bird and placed it in their car. As they started to drive off, several local men stood in the road and prevented their leaving. When the pair said they were driving the bird to the Audubon Society Camp at Walpole, the suspicious local fellows said "Okay," but followed the pair to the camp. The eaglet was returned safely to its nest later in the day by a federal wildlife official.

Each winter, those who observed and kept an eye out for the welfare of this fragile eagle family faced the awful question: Will they make it back in the spring?

That this pair continued to thrive for two decades was a relief and delight to the Hatches and their Damariscotta Mills neighbors. Efforts were made to further protect the eagles from harassment or danger. The owner of the land on which the nest tree was located signed an agreement with the US Fish and Wildlife Service designating the nest and its surroundings as a wildlife sanctuary, and signs warned people away. By federal law, it is illegal to approach closer than six hundred feet from the nest tree.

But even with these precautions, life was full of constant perils and travails for the eagles. There were other incidents of shooting near the nest. Curiosity seekers, ignoring the signs, trampled about the point of land under the nest, causing the eagles great distress and alarm. Once, we received a shock when a fisherman reported finding one of the adult eagles shot to death on an island in the lake. On investigation it turned out, fortunately, to be a great blackbacked seagull.

The eagles occupied this nest continuously for over twenty years. This placed them at the point of old age. There was the possibility these were not the same eagles which originally built the nest at this location. Eagles which have lost a partner to death have been known to return to the nest with a new mate. It was difficult to tell for certain, since it's virtually impossible to live-capture an adult for leg-banding, unlike the young which are banded while still nest-bound.

The Damariscotta Lake eagles produced one or two eaglets each of those years. But how many of their progeny survived in an inhospitable world? The potential hazards were great: gun-happy shooters, steel traps, fishing gear in which to entangle, brutal winter storms, electrocution, starvation.

Yet, despite the overwhelming odds stacked against them during all those years, the eagles of Damariscotta Lake, remnants of a once-dominant species, thrived. They were an irreplaceable treasure, guarded and enjoyed by an entire village.

Part 4:

For the Love of God's Country

18

Perils of a Bush-League Filmmaker

Anything for a Good Outdoors Shot

IT WAS AN UNPLEASANT TASK facing me one evening: cleaning spatters of duck dung from expensive movie camera and tape recorder cases. So I procrastinated by watching TV. I scanned the program listings and discovered that a famous, award-winning filmmaker was being interviewed. Fancying myself a filmmaker of sorts and hoping to learn some new tricks, I tuned in.

The spot opened with a clip of the star's prizewinning movie: out-of-focus lights, tilted-angle shots of modern buildings and sculptures, and other wonders of modern art. This was all scored with a soundtrack of pulsating psychedelic electronic music and street interviews of "just plain folks" sharing their conceptions of "What Art Is."

The reporter asked the filmmaker about his work. Here was a youngish, modish, articulate, highly educated, sophisticated man of the world who mingled among the cultural elite. His daily contacts included directors of large museums, presidents of famous colleges and universities, and executives of large movie corporations and television networks.

Inspiring stuff to the young film student, but it only left me depressed at my own shortcomings.

I, too, earned my living by producing movies. But at my level, recognition came hard. Public television network interviewers were definitely not clamoring for my appearance on their shows. And instead of being invited to a jet-set cocktail party, I might spend an evening in my studio, cleaning duck droppings from the leather cases of my equipment.

Photo by Anita Fournier, courtesy of the Maine State Musum

Paul Fournier on assignment on Moosehead Lake to interview Dr. Lee Salk, (right) New York City child psychologist and brother of Dr. Jonas Salk, developer of the Salk Polio vaccine.

Obviously, my life as a film producer had little in common with the interviewee on television. While he spent the day being idolized at the university film school, I spent the day in a thirteen-foot canoe on a Maine duck marsh.

And whereas he was the subject of an interview, I was questioning wildlife biology technician Jim Dorso, seated at the other end of our tiny canoe, as he tagged a female wood duck and returned her to her nest with thirteen little white eggs. There was no film crew in evidence, no director or producer, no gaffer, soundman, writer, script person, or gofer. Only Jim and I in our little gear-laden canoe far out on a wild marsh.

But my job had its appeal and compensations. Jim Dorso and I worked on a series of television films produced for the Maine Department of Inland Fisheries and Wildlife in the 1980s and '90s. He was a pleasure to spend time afield with. A big, brawny, soft-spoken woodsman, he knew the lives and habits of nature's creatures as few men did.

On this day we were filming one of Jim's pet projects: checking nesting boxes he had set up in marshes in central Maine for the benefit of wood ducks, once a species in danger of extinction. Aided by the boxes, which take the place of natural nesting cavities in trees removed by logging and land clearing, the woodies responded amazingly well to this care and were becoming abundant again.

Jim delighted in working with his ducks. "There, there, little mother, we won't hurt you," he'd say soothingly as he tenderly removed the hen from her nest, counted her eggs, and affixed a numbered tag to her leg.

The ducks repaid Jim's solicitude by invariably defecating as he removed them from the nest. And in a small canoe, it's hard to keep out of range. Hence, my cleaning chore.

My filming life may not have had the glamour of Hollywood and New York, but it seldom lacked for variety and excitement. One winter I went out to film the annual aerial waterfowl count off the coast of Maine. Thousands of ducks choose to spend the winter on the frigid Atlantic off Maine, rather than flying south to the sun (possibly because they haven't seen those alluring ads). Whatever the reason, they are here, and the federal and state governments conduct flights each winter to count the birds and check on their well-being.

It was a crisp January day with the temperature dipping to 15 below. As an ex–bush pilot, I considered myself a rather blasé flight passenger, figuring I'd seen it all when it came to aerial thrills. I experienced no qualms as I settled myself into the rear seat of our small Cessna aircraft and relaxed to enjoy the flight.

En route to the coast I did an airborne sound and film interview with chief pilot George Later and wildlife biologist Howard "Skip" Spencer, veterans of some fifteen years of these counts. On reaching the wind-torn Atlantic, the flight took on a more exciting tone. Our theater of operations this day was the spectacularly scenic and rugged Mount Desert Island, where mountains and tall headlands plunge into the sea. George dropped the plane to within fifty feet above the water, and began coolly threading our craft among the cliffs, while Skip calmly intoned waterfowl sightings and other data into a tape recorder.

We were traveling at over a hundred miles per hour. Ugly cliffs flashed past our wing tips, while lashing waves grabbed at the wings. Ice floes clogged the bays, and frigid wind blasts slammed our tiny craft. If immersed in the frigid Atlantic, a person would survive for only seconds. Somehow I managed to

keep the camera grinding away and got some good footage . . .
and the closest I ever came to airsickness.

———✕———

One of my more physically demanding assignments was a film
on World Cup ski racing I produced for the State of Maine in col-
laboration with ABC's *Wide World of Sports*. I spent a taxing week in
1971 covering this event at the Sugarloaf Mountain ski area.

With a heavy camera mounted on a body brace, a tape
recorder over my shoulder, and headphones over my ears, I
climbed that Maine mountain innumerable times—sometimes
on skis or ski lifts, sometimes riding snowmobiles and snowcats,
but much of the time walking.

My lens followed skiers through gates; poked into the faces
of timekeepers, gatekeepers, coaches, and officials; captured
the elation of winners and the dejection of losers; and filmed
behind-the-scenes action of equipment preparation, press-
room briefings, and results of tabulations at the feverish race
headquarters. I lost ten pounds that week, and many hours of
sleep in subsequent weeks while editing the film. But I had the
satisfaction of seeing that film selected from among the leading
ski films for continuous screening at the major ski shows.

It's impossible to equate the world of that art-film producer
with mine as a maker of ski films. Not only did I have to protect
myself and my equipment from the hazards of winter conditions, but I also had to cope constantly with balky equipment.
Intense cold slowed down a camera, lenses frosted up, lighting
was tricky, batteries lost power, and brittle film snapped.

Then there was the problem of moving heavy, sensitive,
expensive equipment up and down the mountain. Not to mention following the action of fast-moving racers—who sometimes

hit speeds of 60 to 70 miles per hour—while retaining a smoothness of camera movement that wouldn't render the audience violently motion-sick while they viewed it on the screen.

Big-time film producers had access to gyroscopically controlled camera mounts and lens compensators when filming action scenes. But such exotic and expensive gear was seldom within my budget. So I employed alternative methods.

One of my early ski films was *A Girl, a Mountain, and a Bell*. It showed how a young blind schoolgirl, Jeannette Smith, learned to ski. She conquered the toughest trails by following the sound of a tiny bell on her instructor's ski pole.

For sound, I wired her instructor, Harry Baxter, by concealing a small tape recorder on him (this was before radio mics or digital sound) to catch the voices while they skied.

To shoot one particular angle I wanted—from low in front of the instructor, with his blind student following him down the mountain—I tried several methods. Finally I chose to lie on my back on one of those toboggans used for accident victims, with the camera pointed up and back, and had a ski patrolman steer me down the mountain. I ended up with a big crick in my neck . . . and the shot I wanted.

Sometimes the cameraman himself becomes the object of excitement on the slopes. Such was the case one January when I was covering a Canadian-American ski race for NBC Sports.

A winter rain followed by a severe cold snap had transformed the mountain to almost solid ice—good for ski racers, but bad for lead-footed cameramen. I was using an $8,000 Arriflex camera mounted on a shoulder brace strapped to my body, filming the racers as they came screaming over a sheer headwall, when my feet went out from under me.

To ward off the cold, I had on a pair of insulated skiers' "warm-up" pants, which have an outer covering of smooth nylon. This provided a slick surface. I landed on my bottom and began sliding down the mountainside. I gathered speed down the slope, and shouting spectators were a blur as I went by. My heels finally found a bit of soft snow to dig into, and I stopped at the lip of a deep and tree-studded ravine.

The camera, knocked sideways on its mount, survived the ride unscathed. NBC got its race film. I was unhurt, save for a bruised ego—and posterior. And the wild ride of "that crazy cameraman" superseded many post-race conversations in the valley pubs that evening. Perhaps I should be glad this was before the era of YouTube, or the scene would no doubt have gone viral.

Nearly as exciting were some shooting sessions I had with famous Swiss-born ski acrobat and clown, Ruedi Wyrsch. One of our films, *The Clown Prince*, was shown on the CBS network.

Ruedi was a guy who skied on stilts, fell from chairlifts, wore clown outfits and Charlie Chaplin costumes, and crashed into trees and signposts—all in the interest of fun.

Never a dull moment with Ruedi. He dreamed up his own stunts, once rappelling down the sheer side of the Boston Sheraton Hotel as a publicity stunt, straight into the arms of waiting police, called by startled guests who had seen him climb past their windows. I filmed him while chasing on skis with a handheld camera and a special camera mounted on my helmet. I once used an old-fashioned bobsled to follow him down a mountain.

One of my wilder rides occurred one sunny winter's day when I teamed up with a couple of zany Sugarloaf instructors for a filming sequence. Parker Hall was then Sugarloaf's publicity director. He was a fantastic skier, ski instructor, and ski clown in his own right. Patrick Mouligne, a transplanted ex–ski racer from France (and contemporary of the great Jean-Claude Killy), was director of the Sugarloaf Ski School. A handsome bachelor, he was reputed to be the region's most successful lover.

Patrick was somewhat incapacitated on this day; he had one foot in a cast as the result of a spill on the mountain's steepest headwall. There were those who said Patrick fell while his eye wasn't on the moguls (bumps in the snow) but on a curvaceous female skier instead.

Parker Hall arrived on the mountaintop decked out as a seedy country rube trying to ski for the first time. We wanted to show him as a neophyte racing downhill at breakneck speed and repeatedly avoiding disaster by scant inches. In order to avoid a faked look resulting from much film cutting and editing, we wanted to show it all in one take—a tough assignment, since Parker's run would cover a long stretch of the mountain.

That's when Patrick showed up, riding a snowmobile, and offered me a ride. So it was that two crazy Frenchmen went hurtling down that mountain, one wearing a cast and driving, the other (I am of French-Canadian descent) seated backwards and keeping the camera running and aimed at Parker as he followed within a few feet of us. He weaved from side to side on the trail and occasionally even ahead of us, losing along the way his ski poles, gloves, and hat. His pants slipped down to reveal bright red flannel underwear, and he ended up skiing backwards into a big, bushy spruce tree. This one continuous take seldom fails to bring down the house.

You might think that all of this excitement and adventure during "normal" working hours would be enough for most folks. But my late wife Anita and I, both born-and-bred Mainers, loved nothing better than spending our leisure time camping out in the woods and filming and recording wildlife—not only birds and insects and wildflowers, but also deer, eagles, moose, and bears.

Most of these were pleasant interludes, as we spied on wild mothers nursing their babes, or birds teaching their young to fly.

There was the time we found a huge, heavy-antlered bull moose standing up to his shoulders in a trout pond and feeding on underwater plants. Crouched in the bow of our canoe as I filmed, I kept urging Anita to ease us closer with the paddle each time the forest monarch lowered his head underwater for a fresh mouthful. Each time the moose raised his head and shook water from his wide-spreading antlers, Anita would stop paddling.

"Closer, closer!" I stage-whispered, until I heard my wife draw her breath in fear and mutter, "My God, you're insane!"

Only then did I look out from behind the camera lens to find myself staring right into the bull's mean eyeball, as the hackles on his back rose menacingly and water dripped from his nose practically onto the front of my lens. We hurriedly back-paddled to deeper water.

Old man moose, roused to anger at this intrusion, splashed ashore in a welter of flying spray. Spying a younger bull feeding innocently nearby, the monarch lowered his menacing rack and charged him instead of us, sending the youngster scrambling into the woods. The old bull vented his anger on a clump of bushes, snorting and ripping with his antlers until he reduced the brush to shreds. Then he strolled regally into the forest, casting a sidelong glance in our direction as he left. We had learned our lesson, thereafter giving this old fellow, and others like him, a wide berth.

On another pond we once edged closer and closer to a large feeding cow moose trailing a weeks-old calf. We were shooting some great footage when the cow snorted in alarm and splashed out beyond our canoe, placing us between her and her calf. This was potentially even more dangerous than the situation with the bull: A threatened cow separated from her calf can be unpredictable. There were a few tense moments as mama raised her hackles and began nervously running out her long, red tongue—apparently a sign of moose tension.

Fortunately, the spindly-legged, honey-blond calf chose to ignore us and swam out to meet its mother, providing us with some good shots as the two swam across to the solitude of a quiet cove to resume their feeding. We left them alone.

Once a bear approached where I was hiding on the side of a trail, hoping to photograph deer. After a time just a few feet separated us, and I was looking for a tree to climb. The bear became aware of my presence and fortunately bolted for the tall timber.

It's doubtful that prestigious filmmakers from the citadels of movie art would find much in common with this rough-and-tumble level of cinematic work.

Yet in terms of enjoyment and pleasure, I think I hold an edge. I happen to think that filming the natural world is a form of art, a unique challenge. There's poetry in a young skier challenging an awesome mountain, a canoeist riding white water, or a heavy-antlered moose swimming majestically across a wilderness pond.

There's also the sure knowledge that these arty sophisticates will never experience the sheer glow of self-pride that follows from having cleaned duck spatters from a leather camera case, restoring it to its original sleek beauty.

19

The Fight That Never Was

The Night Clay and Liston Boxed in Lewiston

MAY, 1965. THE NATION WAS STILL IN RECOVERY, reeling in shock from the assassination of John F. Kennedy barely a year and a half earlier. In Vietnam, American soldiers were dying in the jungles, and President Johnson was on the verge of doubling the draft, from 17,000 to 35,000 inductees per month. College campuses were seething scenes of rioting, screaming, tie-dyed protestors. The entire world, it seemed, had turned topsy-turvy.

Even in remote, slumbering, somewhat detached Maine, we were experiencing the first rumblings of an approaching tempest. The tiny industrial city of Lewiston had somehow, inexplicably, unfathomably, been selected as the unlikely site for the next Cassius Clay / Sonny Liston World Heavyweight Boxing Match.

(Clay, though he had already adopted the Muslim name, Muhammad Ali, was not yet being universally accepted as such. The sports press still insisted upon calling him Cassius. For some obscure reason, some had even hung upon him the appellation "Gaseous Cassius.")

Why Lewiston and not Vegas, or Reno, or New York, or some other exotic center of glamour and glitz—and money? If there was a rational explanation at the time, it was not forthcoming. Or dimming memory over the past decades has spirited it away. No rationale would seem credible; it simply made no sense. But it was coming, nonetheless.

This was during a time when professional boxing, though highly suspect, still retained some shred of respectability. The glory days of boxing, as exemplified by former champs Jack Dempsey, Gene Tunney, and Joe Louis, were fondly remembered. The prize fights formerly brought to us via radio, which had kept millions glued to their sets on fight nights, had now been usurped by the still-young and burgeoning age of black-and-white television. The Friday Night Fights perennially sponsored by Gillette were among the biggest draws of network sports programming, although some of boxing's luster was starting to tarnish. Though not an avid boxing fan (unlike my father, who seldom missed a Friday night watching the flickering TV images, no matter how obscure and lowly ranked the pugilists), I was inexorably drawn into the gathering maelstrom. As the sports editor on a small Maine daily newspaper, the *Bath Daily Times*, my beat was covering and editing sports. So I was soon besieged daily by press releases, phone calls, and personal visits from what apparently was a small army of frenetic publicists angling for copy space on our sports pages.

This somewhat ardent wooing for my attention was alternately interesting, flattering, amusing, and annoying. But there were compensations. For one, celebrities began drifting into Maine.

First of these was Bath's own Shirley Povich, sports columnist for the *Washington Post*, and one of the world's most widely read and respected sportswriters. Povich had grown up in Bath, graduating from local Morse High School in 1922. He spent several days prior to the fight staying with relatives in the area, and graciously allowed his picture to be taken for our sports section.

Another sportswriting celeb with local ties who made an appearance was Axford Buck, famed boxing writer for the *New York Post*. Known as "Al" to the sports world, he was remembered as "Bill" when he grew up in Day's Ferry, across the Kennebec River from Bath.

These were the leaders of a small army of some five hundred newsmen from all over the world who were converging on our state for the fight. Naive Maine had never seen the like. Most were staying at the famous, sprawling Poland Spring Resort Hotel west of Lewiston, where Liston had set up his training camp.

According to an Associated Press story we ran, many of the world press admitted they were coming because ". . . they were still trying to figure out the bizarre happenings of fifteen months ago" when Clay had won the title away from Liston in a puzzling and controversial way. At the prefight weigh-in to that Miami fight, Clay's pulse had galloped from 54 to 190, prompting the attending doctor to state, "This is a man who is scared to death. He is living in mortal fear." Some witnesses doubted Clay would even show up for the fight.

That fight, described as weird and unique, surprisingly found Clay deftly outboxing the favored Liston for the first four rounds. Then Clay unexpectedly tried to quit, claiming he was blinded by an irritant—liniment allegedly placed on Liston's gloves. When the fight resumed, Liston, undefeated in twenty-eight fights and rated unbeatable, suddenly quit. He remained seated in his corner after the sixth round. Both his eyes were swollen, and he had a gash under the left eye. He claimed he had injured his left shoulder.

And Cassius Clay, aka Muhammad Ali, was the new Heavyweight Champion of the World, if somewhat under a cloud of suspicion.

Maine had its first opportunity to meet many of the boxing world celebrities at a lobster- and clambake for reporters, photographers, and other important types held at Reid State Park on the coast near Bath.

As one account of the affair put it, "Damon Runyon would have loved it. Probably never have Maine people seen so many typically Runyonesque characters in one place on the Maine coast."

The cookout was held in a large, gaily striped tent set up close to the ocean. A heavy overcast sky and haze in late afternoon dissipated as the clambake got under way, and the wind died, making the evening near-perfect. The tide was almost full at early evening, and surf was breaking handsomely over the rocks and sandy beaches to lend natural beauty to the festive occasion.

The place was alive with personalities—and characters. The line of hungry people filing past clambake master Red McMann and his crew of servers, busy handing out Maine lobsters and clams, corn on the cob (from Florida), hot dogs, chicken, etc., was a walking who's who of the sports world.

Showing great gusto at putting away some of McMann's seaweed-and-smoke-flavored shellfish were two former heavyweight champs and one top contender—all obviously not in training at the moment.

The two ex-champs were Jimmy Braddock, who held the title in the pre–Joe Louis era and was now a tall, straight, white-haired sixtyish gentleman; and Jersey Joe Walcott, ageless and jovial and looking tough enough to climb into the ring with either of the current title seekers. Joe was generally conceded to be the Maine Boxing Commission's choice as the referee for next Tuesday night's Clay-Liston fight.

George Chuvalo, the Canadian heavyweight king, was there with his manager, Irving Ungerman. The pair had just thrown down the gauntlet at Liston's training camp, offering to take him on, win or lose, later in the year.

A disappointment to many was the failure of Joe Louis to appear. He was expected aboard one of the buses from Poland Springs, but he didn't make it. It was later learned that he had played thirty-six holes of golf on the famous Poland Spring course and came off too late to make the bus. (I met and photographed Joe the following day in Poland Springs, when he graciously took a few minutes away from golf to meet the press. He came across as a modest, quiet, and dignified gentleman.)

Making a particular impression at the clambake was a group of British sports scribes, some sporting long, flowing locks and handlebar mustaches   exotics in Maine at the time. One of the more flamboyant was Desmond Hackett of the *London Daily Express*. There were also reporters from Sweden, Germany, France, and other countries. Seeing the scenic coast of Maine and experiencing lobsters and clams Down East style for the first time, their comments ran to: "Marvelous! Wonderful! Great!"

I knew the clambake master, Edward J. "Red" McMann, well. He was a local Bath businessman and member of the Bath City Council. The stubby, rotund, ever-jolly McMann stayed as busy as an ant on a hot griddle. He kept four roaring birchwood fires going and ran from them to serving line to feeding tent as he masterminded a small army of helpers. McMann was also frequently called upon by various press and promotional photographers to pose with dignitaries. But he remained characteristically un-awed by his distinguished guests. He was an old hand at this, after having staged big bakes at the New York World's Fair and the Mets' Shea Stadium.

In a quiet moment at the end of the feast, McMann told me that he had fed an estimated 400 guests that evening. He had cooked 760 lobsters, 50 chickens, 9 bushels of clams, 48 dozen ears of corn, and 70 pounds of hot dogs. He had brewed 25 gallons of coffee in old-fashioned copper boilers. And presumably he'd made 400 new friends for the state of Maine.

———✕———

As darkness descended on Reid State Park and the buses and cars laden with well-sated guests wended their way out of the park gate, talk and anticipation turned toward the heavyweight fight three evenings hence, on Tuesday, May 25.

As a member of the sports press, I'd been given a pass providing access to all parts of the fight's venue, the Central Maine Youth Center in Lewiston. This meant I'd have the opportunity to roam at will. I was not permitted, however, at immediate ringside, which was reserved for the scribes and photographers from the leading media sources.

That was fine with me. They had the expertise to provide the blow-by-blow minutiae of the fight itself. My interest ran more to observing and photographing the crowd, the atmosphere, the ambiance of this exotic affair.

In addition to the press pass, I had a reserved-seat ticket, "in case you want to bring along your wife or a friend." The ticket, valued at $100 (approximating a week's pay for a working stiff or news reporter at the time), was for choice seating only a few rows back from ringside. My wife expressed no interest, but I knew someone who would relish the opportunity: my boxing-aficionado father. As we drove to the fight arena that Tuesday evening, Dad was characteristically quiet, but I could sense his suppressed excitement. He was like a kid on Christmas morning.

When we arrived, the Central Maine Youth Center was filling rapidly to its 4,900-seat capacity. After seeing Dad to his seat, I began moving about, casing the joint. Scaffolding had been erected along one entire wall, and it was lined with a battery of film and television news cameras. The fight, we'd been informed, would be televised by closed-circuit to arenas throughout the country, where paying customers sat expectantly. Powerful television lights glared over the ring and spilled out across the audience, darkening gradually toward the walls. Ringside was surrounded with cameramen, still photographers, reporters at their portable typewriters and teletype machines, and newscasters at their microphones. The noise level rose as people talked excitedly, and shouting vendors plied the aisles.

The scene was both festive and raucous. The audience itself was rather unusual for Maine: a liberal sprinkling of expensively styled suits, elaborately coiffed and bejeweled female companions, burly, cigar-chomping males, and a smattering of faces of color—all rarities in 1960s Maine.

The evening got off to a bizarre start when a young but soon to become famous crooner named Robert Goulet climbed into the ring to sing the national anthem. The French-Canadian performer had been invited because his roots befitted Lewiston's large Franco-American population. But he simply did not know "The Star-Spangled Banner," and evidently had not rehearsed. He had dined that evening with Governor John Reed and apparently had imbibed much of his meal. As many in the audience concluded: "He was soused."

Goulet thoroughly mangled the anthem, singing off-key to the accompanying organ. His slurred rendition included parts that sounded like ". . . dawn's early night," and "gave proof through the fight." It set the stage for the events to follow.

Then it was time for the ring announcer to introduce the fighters. Clay almost danced down the aisle, waving and clowning and smiling as he approached the ring. In sharp contrast, Liston's approach was zombie-like. I was standing close to the aisle, and he passed within a few feet of me. I was shocked. Here was a man who days before had been declared one of the finest-conditioned and trained athletes in the world.

Yet he emerged from his dressing room looking like a deathly sick man. His eyes stared glassily, and he bumped blindly into persons lining his route to the ring. And when he removed his robe, his body was beaded and dripping with perspiration. I've always since wondered at his condition: Was he drugged? Semi-paralyzed with fear? Actually sick? Who knows?

Finally the bell rang, and the much-anticipated, much-balleyhooed fight was on—and over!

The thousands of fight fans in the arena that night and a television audience of millions witnessed an event that may well have sounded the death knell of the glory of the once-great sport of boxing.

In one minute flat of the first round of a "fight" that saw little but a demonstration of boxing dances and light feints and jabs, some from as far as six or eight feet away, they watched a man who had been working for a year to reach the peak of proficiency apparently stumble to his knees, roll lazily onto his back while a crazed opponent danced a jig around his body, and then get up and fight without benefit of a referee for five or six seconds before being declared the loser. The referee (yes, Jersey Joe Walcott), meanwhile, was gazing out over the crowd, and the timekeeper was counting Liston out.

The arena was bedlam. The fans, many of them clutching the stubs of $100 tickets, could only find satisfaction for what most figured was a first-class fleecing by jumping up and screaming "Fix!" and "Fake!"

If the local fans were confused, they were in good company. I reached ringside seconds after the "knockdown," and there the hundreds of knowledgeable fight reporters were apparently as dazed and confused by the weird doings as were we natives. Many were arguing among themselves. Among all there was one basic point of argument: Some said they had seen a "phantom punch" hit Liston; most said they had not.

Within seconds, the ring was crowded with shouting fight reporters, hangers-on, and policemen trying to restore order and prevent a general riot. Many fans merely stood on their chairs (my father included) in shock and numbly watched the strange proceedings in the jammed, riotous ring where Clay continued yelling and threatening to reopen the fight against the wobbly Liston.

The Associated Press reported the end thusly: "Clay pressed the scowling Liston, stalking and moving in. Then suddenly, Clay lashed out with an overhand right that traveled only a few inches.

"The massive 215 1/4-pound Liston thumped to the canvas like a stricken ox. He lay there a moment, then tried to get to his feet only to fall back again.

"[Referee] Walcott appeared confused. He looked around dazedly for the timekeeper. Then he hovered over Liston.

"When Liston fell back a second time, Walcott walked to the edge of the ring. Liston rose and the fight continued—in a state of chaos. Clay belted the challenger three times before Walcott rushed in to end the fight.

"Then [ring announcer] Johnny Addie went to the microphone and announced: 'The winner and still champion—Muhammad Ali. The time: one minute.' "

There was, of course, plenty of post-fight rehashing, blaming, and finger-pointing. Even the time was questioned. Some claimed up to one minute, forty-five seconds. The chairman of the Maine Boxing Commission, George Russo, said it was one minute flat, and was quoted as stating that "there was nothing suspicious about the fight." (Some questioned his eyesight.) Liston later said that he was waiting for Walcott's count, which he never heard. "I could have got up, but I didn't hear the count," he complained.

The timekeeper, McDonough, placed the blame for the confusion on Walcott, who was looking at the crowd and never at him. Walcott contended he was trying to get Clay into a neutral corner, and was depending on the timekeeper to continue the count. And McDonough was also quoted as saying, "If that bum Clay had gone into a neutral corner instead of running around like a maniac, all the trouble would have been avoided."

Apparently not all the fight action was confined to Lewiston. The media reported that fights broke out at several closed-circuit arenas around the country. In Albany, New York, a scuffle erupted between two men when one complained the other had stood up with the comment, "Your head was in my way and I missed the whole thing." The biggest brawl of all was at the Cleveland arena, where 5,404 paying fans became distraught before the fight started when the venue ran out of beer.

In Maine, dreams of becoming another fight capital were dashed. It had hoped for a world-class sporting event. It received—and became—a joke.

I just wish Dad could have gotten to see, in person, one major-league boxing match in his lifetime.

20

Frenzy in the Woods

The Media Goes Hunting

A "FLAG" IS THE UPRAISED WHITE TAIL of an alarmed deer, which they use to alert other deer of danger. A certain number of ignorant, overanxious, or downright stupid hunters have been known to shoot when they spot such a flag, in the vain hope of hitting the deer. At best, it's a lousy shot. It can only result in wounding the deer in the hindquarters, which usually allows it to get away but later suffer a lingering death in some hidden thicket.

Such an alleged flag shot resulted in one of the most tragic, sensationalized hunting accidents in Maine history. It made national news.

A young, attractive mother and two infants were ensconced in their house in a new development near the city of Bangor. She and her husband, an assistant professor at a nearby college, were "from away." That is, they had recently moved to Maine from another state and were unfamiliar with rural traditions—and hunting. When she saw armed hunters enter the woods near her home, the woman, evidently fearful for the safety of her children, left the house and went out to warn the hunters to stay away.

Unfortunately, the reporters who responded to the scene almost as quickly as rescuers and investigators got the initial story only partially correct. Soon it was being spread like wildfire. The headlines screamed, and the airwaves reverberated:

YOUNG MOTHER SHOT AND KILLED IN HER YARD BY HUNTER
WHILE PROTECTING HER BABIES!

The reporters, of course, had not been allowed to the actual scene, which was sealed off to protect it from evidence contamination while it was being investigated. So unfortunately they went with assumptions and scanty hard facts.

Even after I, a public information officer for the state Fish and Wildlife Department at the time, released the real story, the sensational original persisted. It had a life of its own and fed on a wave of anti-hunt frenzy. The image portrayed was of a woman, standing heroically on her manicured lawn amid sandboxes and swing sets, gunned down by a blood-lusting hunter. The story fed on emotion. I saw one television reenactment of the incident which showed that very scenario.

During the nearly twenty years I was employed as media coordinator for the Maine Department of Inland Fisheries and Wildlife (including the Maine Warden Service), I dealt on a daily basis with the members of the press. Our relations were, for the most part, excellent. I gave them what I believed was the straightest and most complete information possible. The only times I ever recall that we ran into "difficulties" was during the fall hunting season. This would cause me days of stress and grief, exacerbated by the fact that officers investigating a scene are usually loathe to release details while the investigation is ongoing. Premature release of information can jeopardize a case. Sometimes not much is sure until certain forensic tests have been concluded.

To some members of the media, this simply meant that we were withholding or covering up the true facts in order to put the best light on the situation.

I must admit that there were some in our department who did not want to make anything public. My response to them was this: "If you don't give out the information, they will assume the worst-case scenario and report it their way, which will likely make it appear worse than it really is."

One department employee (not a warden) who mistrusted the media and was resisting my efforts to get some information from him, once accused me, "You're one of them!" In his mind, "them" was the lowest of the low. He had gotten in trouble with the media, and said he had been "burned" by them before I had come aboard.

I happened to be in a plane the afternoon of the shooting incident, flying over Merrymeeting Bay with chief pilot Dana Toothaker and wildlife educator Lisa Kane. We were filming concentrations of ducks in the bay when word came over the radio to go to a small town west of Bangor to shoot aerial photos of a hunting accident. In less than an hour we were there and communicating with the investigating wardens on the ground.

The scene was a recently logged-over piece of ground near some newly built upscale houses on a dead-end road. Wardens had been stationed at the spot where the shooter had stood, and where the victim had been hit. We made a number of passes over the scene and shot still photos and video footage.

Until we landed, those of us in the plane hadn't known any of the particulars. But now we began learning the full impact of this tragic story. Sad as the shooting was, the media portrayal of the incident was not a true picture.

I went to the scene on the ground, and met the man in charge of the case, warden investigator (equivalent to detective) Gary Sargent. Gary needed official photo documentation of the scene. I set up still and video cameras at the exact spot where the victim had stood, and shot pictures and videotape of a warden standing where the shooter had been.

I then reversed and shot from the shooter's position toward the victim's. Rather than being on her lawn, the woman had actually walked through a strip of woods behind her home to the edge of the logged area. From the shooter's position, the house was not visible, screened by a buffer strip of woods separating the house from the "chopping" (logged area). And the hunter had been well beyond the thousand-foot legal safety zone from the house. These were the facts—facts that the frenzied media ignored.

This still did not exonerate the shooter, of course. The first rule of hunting safety is to be sure of your target. The woman, unfortunately and tragically, had made a big mistake. In her naiveté and ignorance of Maine woods protocol, she was wearing a pair of mittens—*white* mittens—which she was waving in an effort to wave off the hunter.

The allegation presented to the grand jury was that the hunter had made that fatal error. He had made a "flag shot."

The hunter insisted he had seen and fired at a deer. However, the investigating wardens, who scoured the ground minutely, found no tracks or other signs deer had been there. In fact, it seemed unlikely that deer would have been so close to a human.

The hunter was indicted for negligent manslaughter based on the evidence, including photo and video documentation, presented by Gary Sargent. A trial date was set. The story kept cropping up in various places while speculation and arguments raged among pro- and anti-hunt proponents. It looked like a slam-dunk for the antis—an open-and-shut case for a conviction.

But astonishingly, when the jury came in, it acquitted the hunter. The prosecution's carefully, meticulously documented and presented case failed.

The hunter, well-known, respected, and liked, was spared by a jury of his peers who evidently could not believe such a nice person could have done anything as bad as portrayed. Perhaps exhibiting some anti-outsider bias, they felt the woman was at least partially culpable. She should not have left her home and, in their view, virtually committed suicide by waving those white mittens in the woods during deer season.

Every Maine hunter learns that you never wear white in the deer woods during open season. In fact, hunters don't use white handkerchiefs, and even carry red toilet paper.

***

One of the most trying of my efforts with the media dragged out over an entire weekend. It was no fault of anyone within our department.

I received a call on a Friday afternoon from one of the warden sergeants that there had been a hunting fatality south of Damariscotta. All he knew at the moment was that a hunter had been found dead. Wardens had secured the scene and were protecting it from contamination, but they could do nothing until the body was examined by a pathologist from the state medical examiner's office.

"No need to rush about getting here," said the sergeant. "The assistant ME [medical examiner] who's on duty today says she'll be tied up for a few hours before she can get down here from Augusta."

I dutifully put out a notice to the wire services that we had an unattended death of a hunter, but no further details were available. In early evening I drove down to the location. I arrived to find several deputy sheriffs directing traffic and trying to corral a group of angry, impatient television crews who had been forbidden from entering the woods and approaching the death scene.

Once they spotted me I was surrounded by cameras, lights, and microphones. I said we had nothing to report until the medical examiner visited the scene and gave us the go-ahead. Nothing I said appeased them.

I took a flashlight and proceeded down a beaten path through the snowy woods. After a few hundred yards I could hear a generator running ahead, and soon could see the garish lights loaned by the local fire department through the tree branches.

Protective yellow tape surrounded a small clearing, and several wardens stood around the perimeter, talking quietly. They nodded hello at my arrival.

In the middle of the bright area was the object of interest. The body of a fairly heavy man, clad in hunting clothing, lay facedown in the several inches of snow on the ground. No visible wounds were evident, nor could I see a firearm. The man's arms were under his body. A pool of congealing, freezing blood spread from around the head.

As I stood there, Dan Murray, a warden I knew, came out of the woods with a flashlight and stood near me. I asked what he'd been doing. He replied he'd just walked completely around the site, looking for tracks or signs anyone had approached near. He found none. Whatever happened had occurred right here. I returned to the roadside. When the doctor arrived, I escorted her by flashlight. She was a diminutive, slim woman with a quiet, intense demeanor. At the scene, she stood silently at the perimeter for long moments, her eyes roving and study- ing everything. She looked intently at the ground, the sur- rounding trees, even up into the tree branches. She slowly walked completely around the body, examining from all angles. She carefully removed small pieces of matter from tree branches and placed them into plastic bags.

She finally motioned. Several wardens approached and care- fully rolled the body onto its back. The sight shocked us to our boots.

Dan Murray exclaimed, "Jeez! He's got no face left!" Indeed, where the face should have been was a mass of meat and bone. The rifle was still clutched in his arms, pointed up toward the head. There was no doubt in any of our minds: This poor guy had taken his own life.

The doctor instructed the wardens to place the body in a body bag and was ready for me to escort her back to her vehicle. I asked if it was all right now to release the information that this was a self inflicted death and not a hunting accident. She hesitated and said she preferred to wait until she had performed the postmortem. There were still some things she wanted to determine, and she said the autopsy could not be performed until Sunday. This left me on the hook to deal with the press corps for the remainder of the weekend. Not a pleas- ant prospect, especially since the facts of the incident seemed so certain.

It is customary—indeed, mandatory—that a warden be pres- ent at the postmortem. It's one of the more unpleasant aspects of the job. I made arrangements with the designated warden to call me as soon as possible after the doctor gave him the okay, so I could release the news and call off the slavering hounds of the media.

And salivating they were. My phone rang all weekend. "Who's the shooter?" "Has there been an arrest yet?" "How soon can you tell us?" And on and on. Even though I knew the answer that would cool them, I couldn't say it.

Finally, by mid-afternoon on Sunday, the call came from the warden. He'd just left the autopsy room. He sounded a bit peaked. It hadn't been a pleasant morning for him.

"Okay," he said. "She's all done."

"Did she say to go ahead and release the information?"

"Yup. I gotta run. See you around." And he hung up.

With a mental sigh of relief I sent out the call and released the information that the doctor had termed it a self-inflicted gunshot.

Not long after, I received a call from a reporter from a Portland television station. "I just talked with the doctor to get more details, and she says she never released that information."

"What? I got that from the warden who was there, and he assured me she had approved the release." I mulled this over for a moment and then said, "Let me try to contact her. I'll get right back to you!"

I called the medical examiner's number. Fortunately, the doctor answered. I explained what had happened, and she replied:

"Yes, I just spoke with that reporter. I'm not quite finished. There are some more lab tests I'd like to complete, and that will take at least several more days."

I could hardly contain my frustration. Evidently so deeply engrossed in her science, she was oblivious to the media storm

swirling out there. As patiently as I could, I explained to her
what we were up against. The media, instead of sticking to facts,
were playing with innuendo and speculation—all negative.
Finally I asked her, "Is there any chance it could be anything
other than having his head blown off that finished his life?"

At length she agreed that she was 99 percent sure. She
finally agreed to releasing a statement that the death was
"consistent with a self-inflicted gunshot wound." At last, I could
wiggle off the hook.

⬤━✕━⬤

Thanksgiving weekend is one the Maine Warden Service
always sweats out. It's the final weekend of the Maine deer-
hunting season, which ends on that Saturday. Hunters who still
haven't "filled their tags" (i.e., shot and tagged a deer) are out in
force. The pressure is on. It's now or never. The atmosphere is
ripe for "incidents." In Maine, only about one in seven or eight
licensed hunters tag a deer in a normal season.

My home phone began ringing about 7:30 the morning
of a Thanksgiving Saturday. Reporters, tuned in to their radio
scanners, had heard a snatch of a transmission, apparently from
a warden plane to a ground search party. The location was an
unincorporated, or "wild," township east of Rangeley Lake.

A ground search had been under way there during the night
for a man overdue from hunting the previous day. There was
light snow on the ground. The missing hunter had failed to
respond to signal shots fired during the night. A warden plane
piloted by Dana Toothaker had been called out at daybreak.

Low clouds hung over the landscape and snow threatened.
The pilot had only a brief window of opportunity to search.
What the reporters heard over the radio was the pilot reporting

that he could see the man lying on the ground in a small opening along a woods road. The man's tracks led up to where he
fell, and there was no sign he had moved after falling. A light
snow had fallen during the night, and the man's clothes were
lightly dusted. He appeared to be dead.

That was the only transmission heard. Evidently the pilot
had to leave immediately as the weather was worsening.
Ground-party radio transmissions could not be picked up. The
search area was north of the chain of Appalachain Mountains,
which blocked radio signals. The plane radio call had no doubt
been heard because it was aloft, and perhaps using the so-called
"statewide" radio channel which uses repeater stations to reach
wide areas. Ground wardens would no doubt be talking to each
other on the "local" channel with limited range, especially on
portables.

These events made it impossible for me to reach anyone
for information. Our regional headquarters were closed for the
holiday weekend. No warden-service dispatchers were on duty.
I even tried the state police dispatchers, who were provided
with warden service frequencies. They could make no contact.
Even cell phones, still rare at the time, likely would not have
worked so far from any towers.

So we all waited. My phone was seldom silent, and it could
not be ignored. Each call could have been the one from a
warden with the information I needed. I was on the hot seat for
most of that frustrating day, at the mercy of the media. From
past experience I knew it would be a long day. Nothing could
be done until a medical examiner had gone to the scene and
made a preliminary determination as to the cause of death.

And, as usual, in the absence of solid information, reporters
were assuming someone had been shot.

It wasn't until very late in the afternoon that a state police dispatcher called to say the wardens were out of the woods and had "signed out" at a restaurant in Rangeley. I asked the dispatcher to make contact and have a warden call me with information ASAP.

It still took a while—these guys had been out in the cold, snowy woods probably all night and day. They were tired and deserved to have a hot meal. At last a warden sergeant called me with the news.

This hunter, a young man in his twenties, had suffered for years with some obscure disease. It apparently struck him down in mid-stride. "He just fell right there, and you could tell from the marks in the snow that he never moved again. Must have died instantly."

I thanked the sergeant and suggested he go home and get some rest. I was finally able to get the word out to the press that it was a simple, unattended death. It was amazing how quickly they lost interest.

I hope I haven't left the impression that hunting is deadly dangerous. Far from it.

Bear in mind that these are isolated incidents, compressed from nearly twenty years of observation. In fact, during my time at IF&W, the number of hunting accidents dropped precipitously. This can be attributed to two factors: the introduction of mandatory wearing of fluorescent blaze-orange outerwear visible from all sides, and hunter-safety courses, now required for all new hunters before obtaining a hunting license for the first time, and for anyone who has not held a license during the past ten years.

These measures have proved effective, even life-saving. Whereas at one time Maine experienced as many as sixty to seventy hunting accidents and fifteen to nineteen fatalities annually, by the time I retired in the late 1990s, total accidents were fewer than ten. And several of these were of the self-inflicted variety, such as the person's gun accidentally discharging into his foot, or peppering his partner—a la Dick Cheney—with bird shot. For a few seasons there were absolutely no fatalities.

In fact, statistics compiled by researchers show that hunting is one of the safest sports—safer even than fishing or golf.

Strangely enough, as the number of licensed hunters increased and eventually more than doubled, the number of accidents actually dwindled. How to account for this decline?

I like to believe it was due at least in part to the great amounts of hunter-safety messages we kept cranking out to the public via press releases, and perhaps more effectively, to radio and television via public service announcements. There was a constant flow of educational information.

During the late 1940s and '50s, the prevailing attitude among hunters was low visibility. Hunters normally wore dark clothing (a favorite in those pre-camo days was the traditional green-and-black-checkered wool lumberjack shirt as an outer garment), the theory being they could be more successful in fooling deer by blending into the background. Unfortunately, it also fooled too many hunters in mistaking them for game.

Also, many hunters bought guns with which they were unfamiliar, and took them into the woods with little or no training or familiarization. The result was lots of accidental firearm discharges resulting in wounds to themselves or their companions.

The dramatic drop in incidents began during the 1970s. After long promotion and lobbying by hunter-safety advocates—and stubborn opposition by entrenched traditionalist hunters refusing to change their ways—the Maine legislature passed a law forcing mandatory wearing of fluorescent blaze-orange clothing. Almost immediately, there was a sharp drop in the "mistaken-for-game" category of accidents.

No one misses the "bad old days."

In hindsight, in view of the unfortunate young woman who lost her life waving those white mittens, I now recognize that in addition to preaching the message of safety to hunters, we should also have put out information to the uninformed public about the dangers of going into the woods without wearing fluorescent-orange protection. Foresters and woodsmen working in the woods in the fall have learned to do so. It has no doubt saved lives.

21

Have Camera, Will Travel

Stringing for the National Networks

AS SO OFTEN WITH THE GOOD THINGS IN LIFE, my affiliation with
a couple of major TV networks came out of the blue, and the
work grew serendipitously. I had been filming for the US Fish &
Wildlife Service, documenting the early efforts to restore bald
eagles to Maine. NBC was doing occasional one-hour specials
with their star anchorman, David Brinkley. They were covering a story in Maine, needed some wildlife footage, especially
of eagles, and had contacted the USFWS for a source. I got the
referral.

At the time eagles were nearly extinct, and footage was
scarce and difficult to obtain. I sold them not only eagle footage
but also other Maine wildlife stuff I had—moose, deer, bear. It
was a most welcome break.

Back then I also filmed for the Maine ski areas. One day
Harry Baxter, director of the Sugarloaf Ski School, called and
told me of an unusual event coming up: night ski jumping. I got
some good shots of the action on the well-lighted impromptu
ski jump and of the fun-loving crowd.

Emboldened by my recent success with wildlife footage,
I called the executive producer at NBC and described what I

had. I sent the ski film and story down to New York. A day or so later a nice check arrived and the story appeared on the *NBC Nightly News*. The following day I received a telegram (yes, a quaint telegram) from a high executive at the network thanking me for the story, "which gave our news program a nice lift."

That opened the door. Whenever anything unusual happened at any of the Maine ski mountains—Easter costume parades, races, etc.—I began supplying NBC with footage, for which they paid handsomely. After the ski season I continued to cover other events for them around the state of Maine, which, due to its relative isolation, they had seldom covered.

Once I had an assignment to interview Leon Gorman, grandson of Leon Leonwood Bean and CEO of the giant L.L. Bean corporation. The only time available to him was early in the morning, and the interview had to be shot at the old entrance to the store in Freeport. It was a bitterly cold morning, well below zero.

I got the film and sound equipment set up and waited. Gorman was delayed. My wife Anita (functioning as soundman) and I waited some more, stamping our feet and dancing around to keep from freezing. It must have been forty-five minutes before he emerged. I began filming—and the film, frozen and brittle, began snapping into little pieces in the camera. Needless to say, it ended our shoot for that day.

High-end camera crews got around this problem by encasing the camera in an electrically heated "barney," but I had no such thing. For future shoots, we solved the problem with a homemade barney. The ever-resourceful Anita got some insulated cloth and carefully measured and cut out a shape to fit around the camera. She then sewed it all up, with several pockets inside to hold small hand-warmers. We never had the

Photo by Anita Fournier
Paul Fournier on ski filming assignment for NBC at Jackson Hole, WY.

problem again. (That homemade barney, with a lot of my other film equipment, is now archived at the Maine State Museum.)

Sometime later I again received a call from the NBC producer Shad Northshield. By then he had transferred to CBS, and they were getting ready to launch a new weekly program, *CBS Sunday Morning with Charles Kuralt*. Shad wanted to do a segment for the inaugural program about a planned giant oil refinery proposed for Maine's Quoddy Bay, which has some of the world's highest tides and most treacherous passages for oil tankers. It would endanger Maine's dwindling eagles in the area, and they needed footage. "Grab your best eagle stuff and hop a plane down here," he said. I didn't hesitate.

At the CBS offices in New York, Northshield and his crew and I repaired to an editing room and reviewed the footage. My rare eagle mating sequence made it on the air. They raved over a shot of a young eagle emptying its bowel, which through the telephoto lens made it appear to almost squirt the viewer, but it did not make the final cut.

Northshield hired me as a consultant. A few days later I met a full-fledged camera and producing crew in Augusta. We drove to Washington County and spent a few days shooting scenes, which included taking aerials from a plane. It was my first intro-duction to the inner workings of a network, and I was amazed at their big budget. Need a helicopter? Hire it. A young woman had the job of carrying a big pouch seemingly filled with cash and paid all the expenses. When the crew stopped for dinner at night, she ran an open bar tab. What a way to live for a naive country boy like me.

I developed a friendship with the field producer, Jim Rich-ardson. Jim fell in love with the state of Maine, and was always looking for reasons to come up and do stories. Even after I went to work for the State, he would call and ask, "You got a good story for me?"

Often I did. One was a major piece on biologists captur-ing and radio-collaring adult moose and tagging their calves.

They'd land on water in a float-equipped helicopter. CBS sent up its own helicopter and pilot to chase and film the moose crew at work. I rode their chopper a number of times and became friends with the pilot. In later years, after Jim Richardson had moved on from CBS, that pilot would still occasionally call and ask, "I want to come to Maine. You got a story for us?"

In my network days I also developed a great friendship with Roger Caras. He was a noted author of numerous books, several on nature and animals. An expert on dog breeds, he was, for many years, master of ceremonies at the prestigious Westminster Kennel Club Dog Show.

When I met Roger, he had a national radio program on CBS called *Pets and Wildlife*. He transferred to ABC and became their regular correspondent covering outdoor/wildlife/animal stories. His reports were noted for his great knowledge delivered in a powerful, pleasant baritone. He loved Maine, and jumped at every chance to bring his crew up here, sometimes bringing his wife. We covered numerous subjects, including visiting bear dens in winter to tag the cubs, stories on eagles, moose, etc. I probably collaborated with Roger on more stories than with anyone else in the networks.

For one story we chased around the state by car and helicopter to film the locations where the sun is said to first hit the United States: Was it Eastport? Cadillac Mountain? Mount Katahdin? Mars Hill? He conducted interviews and posed the question to several Maine natives, including some quaint old codgers. It was a delightful piece that aired on ABC's *Good Morning America*.

On another occasion, returning from remote eastern Maine for a story about biologists raising big trout in a secret location, we passed through the village of Lee. Roger and his producer were intrigued by the then-new practice in Maine of setting out "punkin' heads," or stuffed dummies, on lawns, a practice they'd never seen. We spotted a crudely carved wooden head sitting on the porch rail of one house. Roger, ever vigilant for the off-beat, said, "There's gotta be a story there. Let's stop."

The woman who lived in the house told us that the crudely fashioned human head, weathered and abused and spooky, had been carved by her late uncle, a notorious poacher, while he was in jail. As she told it, when the game warden arrived at the man's cabin in the woods, he caught him red-handed with a poached deer. When the warden arrested him, the poacher said, "I ain't moving. You'll have to carry me out!" After some heated "discussion," the warden finally tied the old gent sitting up on a hand sled and hauled him off to jail. The tale was woven into a delightful Halloween piece, with close-ups of the gruesome head and shots of a lonely old graveyard on a gloomy day.

My other association with ABC came about when the World Cup Ski Race was brought to Sugarloaf one winter when the snows failed to fall in the European Alps.

This was a big deal for the state. The top ski racers from all over the world converged on the Maine mountain. Media and spectators came in droves. Ski equipment companies' trucks and vans filled a huge parking lot, where ski techs worked secretly to tune and wax the skis. I was doing ski-promotion filming for the state at the time, and ended up working closely with *ABC's Wide World of Sports* at the event.

The director of the show was a young, bright guy named John Martin. The on-air personalities were Jim McKay and Bob Beattie. While ABC's crack crew of cameramen covered the races, I filmed the behind-the-scenes activity. After the show aired, they provided me and my employer (the State of Maine) with a master of the race coverage, which I combined with my footage to edit into a ski promotional film that was shown widely at ski shows.

Then I got a call from Wayne Hockmeyer. Wayne single-handedly started the whitewater rafting industry in Maine. He was the first to run the roaring waters of the Kennebec Gorge, surprising everyone by living to tell about. I had produced two short promotional films for his growing whitewater business.

Wayne had recently been involved in an *ABC Wide World of Sports* feature filmed on the Kennebec with Ethel Kennedy, wife of Bobby Kennedy, and her children. Wayne had supplied the rafts, guiding, and other services. He felt they had a good show already "in the can," but wanted to supply ABC with some even more spectacular footage.

The company that regulates dams and water power on the Kennebec drainage was about to open the sluiceway at Moxie Pond to drain the lake to allow some work on the dam. This would mean that the small gorge below the dam and above Moxie Falls would be running full bore. This was in late September with the fall foliage nearing its peak—ideal time for dramatic photography. Wayne's plan was to run a kayak through the roaring whitewater gorge and its several waterfalls.

On the appointed day we gathered at the gorge. Wayne had a reputation as a fearless daredevil, and he lived up to it. I had fitted my movie camera with a telephoto lens for a special enhancement technique, called a "compression shot." The long lens, aimed at the right angle, foreshortens a scene so that a waterfall looks steeper than it really is.

Wayne dragged his kayak to the top of the gorge and began his run. The shots looked fantastic through the viewfinder. I was set up at the foot of the biggest, steepest fall when Wayne came sluicing through. Then trouble hit.

Heavy waterfalls often have what is called a "hydraulic" at their foot. To whitewater enthusiasts, this is a well-known and lethal phenomenon. It's sometimes called "The Drowning Machine." Water, plunging down in the pool and flowing out the bottom, creates a backward current at the surface. Rafters, swimmers, boats—whatever gets caught in it are unable to get out. Even rescuers in boats attempting to pick up trapped swimmers have been caught and drowned.

When Wayne hit the base of this waterfall, his kayak got stuck at the bottom. The water rushing down the fall, and the backwash, held the kayak in a death grip. Wayne strained with all his strength but it wouldn't budge. For long moments he struggled. Then his grip weakened and the kayak flipped upside down—still trapped. Wayne's wife Sue was standing next to me. I thought, *We're watching him drown, and there's nothing we can do!* But Wayne was no ordinary man. Suddenly, bracing his paddle against the powerful current, he miraculously righted the kayak. He was still seated in the cockpit, still straining for all he was worth. I couldn't believe what I was seeing. Then he went under again. This time while underwater he bailed out of the kayak.

With his weight removed, the kayak popped down underwater. Both Wayne and his kayak disappeared for a long, breath-stopping moment. Then, far down the long pool, Wayne's head popped up, and an instant later the kayak shot up into the air and settled on the water. Wayne grabbed the rope and managed to pull it to shore, where he collapsed to regain his breath. Then, amazingly, he dragged the kayak to the top of the falls and ran them again! This time he got through the falls and hydraulic successfully. The footage was spectacular.

During these years I was fortunate to do traveling assignments for the networks as well as *Newsweek* magazine's television show—to the Yucatan when it was still wild jungle, to Jackson Hole to film segments on ski races, Yellowstone Park in the winter, and to Ireland and other parts of Europe.

It was all fun, and a welcome addition to the family bank account. But it couldn't last. I was a film guy. When the TV industry transitioned to all video production, I felt too old to make the change. I eventually did, though, and for several years produced a television series on Maine Fish & Wildlife for the state, which aired on the Maine Public Broadcasting Network. It felt like coming home.

22

His Name Was "Nuge"

A Living Legend in the North Woods

I WAS TWENTY YEARS OLD, flying my small Piper Cub seaplane around the Allagash Wilderness Region of northern Maine, when a bad turn of weather forced me to find a safe haven. It turned out to be a remote, isolated "sporting camp" actually a collection of primitive log cabins—located on the east shore of Chamberlain Lake. Here, some sixty miles from the nearest town and highway, as I sat out the storm, I was graciously welcomed in and had the great pleasure of meeting Alan and Patty Nugent.

During that weather-induced stay, we determined that as I was a registered guide looking for work, and as the Nugents would be needing some guiding assistance during the upcoming deer-hunting season, when they would be hosting parties of hunters from New York, I should work for them. So began a friendship that would endure for the next three decades.

It didn't take long for me to discover the strength of this gentle giant of the North Woods. At six-foot-plus and some 240 pounds, in his prime "Nuge," as he was known throughout northern Maine, would probably have put most NFL linebackers to shame. I was there several days before the first hunting party arrived, which he and I spent in routine camp chores in preparation.

One of the never-ending demands around a Maine sporting camp is putting up firewood. Sports, as clients are called in Maine, love to burn wood, and they consume cords of it even when the weather is warm. Plus the Nugents lived in camp all winter and relied solely on wood for heat and cooking. All of this required keeping a couple of big woodsheds filled with drying wood.

So for several days Nuge and I spent time gathering firewood. At that time in the early 1950s, there were no roads, draft animals, or other means of transporting wood from forest to camp. Nuge's answer was a big, ugly, flat-bottomed scow powered by an ancient Johnson outboard motor—the kind you had to wrap a rope around the flywheel to start. It would do so if you were lucky.

In this boat we slowly cruised along the shore looking for suitable trees to cut. The birch trees in that region were suffering from a blight caused by disease or insects. This mostly attacked the upper branches and could be easily spotted. It didn't affect the trunks of most trees, which could be converted into excellent firewood. Our tools were basic: bucksaw, ax, and peavey (aka, cant dog—a rugged wood handle with a spike and swinging hook, or "dog," used for rolling logs).

When we spotted a suitable tree we went ashore, sawed it down, cut it into four-foot lengths, and rassled it into the boat. When we had a boatload we'd run back up to camp to unload. This is when I first saw how rugged this man was.

Once we reached Nugent's cove we began unloading these wood logs onto a wheelbarrow. Green hardwood, still full of moisture, is heavy. When we had a sizable load, I, in a show-off mood, grabbed the handles to wheel it up the embankment to the woodpile. I could barely lift it a few inches. No way could I ever push it up that bank. And I thought I was in pretty good condition—six feet tall but thin, weighing barely 160 pounds.

With a grin and chuckle, Nuge grabbed the handles and pushed that heavy-laden wheelbarrow up the bank and all the way to the woodpile. He was breathing a little heavy, but he just grinned and said, "Jest right."

What an impression I'd made on my first day. But I'd soon learn that Nuge's typical reaction to just about any situation, whether good or hellishly frustrating or bad, was always "Jest right."

<hr />

When I met the Nugents they were in their late forties. Patty Nugent had already established a reputation as an outstanding cook. She created masterpieces of culinary delight and fed large crowds of guests and guides, all from an old-fashioned wood-burning cookstove in the main dining lodge. One of her favorites was corn fritters served with their own maple syrup. It was regular fare at Nugent's Wilderness Camps, and anticipated by all.

One of the highlights of any stay was the after-dinner gathering in the lodge, where Nuge was always the center of entertainment. Sometimes I had to fight off sleep in front of the hot woodstove after spending a long, strenuous day in the outdoors. But some of his tales stuck in my mind.

When there were just the three of us, Nuge alluded to some of his youthful days, apparently filled with adventure. For a time, he lived in the Jackman area, close to Canada, trapping and guiding. This was during the Prohibition era, and the place was notorious for booze smuggling. He never admitted to doing any of that, but he was hired by a "very rich man" to serve as his bodyguard. Apparently when this man sat in on high-stakes card games, Nuge would sit nearby armed with a pistol. No doubt this would be enough to intimidate most would-be cheaters.

During this period Nuge was a trapper. Money was scarce and some furs were valuable. The skin from one fisher or marten might be worth a month's pay. There were some tough characters around and, according to Nuge, "they'd just as soon shoot you as not" to steal your fur or rob your traps. Consequently, trappers like Nugent had to move in secrecy, making sure to not leave trails or tracks, spending days in the woods with just the supplies they could carry on their backs, sleeping under brush piles and eating cold food so as not to have to make fires.

Despite his size, Nuge was a prodigious walker, hiking many miles through the wilderness on snowshoes to tend his traplines. This likely stood him in good stead when he was employed for a time by the Great Northern Paper Company, to clear and maintain miles of telephone lines through the woods—the only link in those pre-radio days to lumber and river-driver camps, dams, and forest ranger stations. The wire, strung from tree to tree, might be blown down by trees or tangled in the antlers of deer or moose and snapped off by their struggles to free themselves.

It was during the Depression-era 1930s, when jobs were unavailable, that Patty and Al made their way to the Allagash Wilderness at Chamberlain Lake. They had no money, but they had an abundance of strength and the guts of pioneers.

They hired a teamster in Patten with a horse-drawn wagon to carry their "wangan," their worldly possessions, including a cookstove, food supplies, and tools, some sixty miles along a woods tote road (a supply trail cleared by lumbermen) to Telos Dam at the foot of Chamberlain. They were accompanied by Patty's brother. They had one dollar between them.

Arriving at Telos, the Nugents built a couple of rafts from logs and attached their only means of power, a two-horse outboard motor, and started up the lake. They could only go when the wind was calm. As Nuge told me, "At times the only way I could tell if we were going forward or back was to line up a couple of trees on the shore and see which way they moved."

In this manner they made their way some dozen miles, across Telos Lake, Round Pond and its Thoroughfare, and into Chamberlain.

For their future home the Nugents chose a tiny cove on the east shore at the mouth of Little Leadbetter Stream. It was just big enough to provide space for landing boats, and to give shelter from the winds and waves on the twenty-mile-long lake.

They had no title, no lease, no legal right to settle on the place. Most of the land around was owned by private paper companies, which tolerated no settlers. But the spot they chose was a public lot, owned by the state of Maine. They became squatters.

Nuge and his brother-in-law put up a crude shelter on the shore from "dri-ki" (driftwood) and set up Patty's cookstove. Good food was essential for the hardworking crew. Patty told me, "I'd set up my flour to make biscuits, and when I'd turn around, the wind would blow it away." She lost several batches that way.

Meanwhile, the two men cleared spaces, cutting trees and dragging them by hand and with rope falls, and began to erect the cabins that would become their home and business for the remainder of their lives.

Nuge was, above all, a very clever engineer of the basics. He was a master at using whatever was at hand to ease the task. He contrived a "gin pole" to use for levering and raising logs and poles for the cabins.

After a few days of strenuous work, misfortune struck. Patty's brother developed an excruciating toothache. They gave him their last dollar and he headed out to find a dentist. The Nugents were left to cope alone.

———

For many years a visit to Nugent's Wilderness Camps gave proof of Nuge's skill and ingenuity. Here was a cluster of snug cabins built of ax-cut logs. The beds you slept in, the table and chairs, even the sinks, were hewn and carved by hand. It was all built with little more than an ax, a saw, a drawknife, and a cant dog—and the sheer strength and ingenuity of one man.

At some point, state officials became aware of the presence of these "squatters" and moved to have them ejected. But this would be no task for the weak-willed. Here was a man with a well-known reputation for great strength and, as he himself admitted, a tough past. He was an expert shot with rifle, shot-gun, and pistol—and he was well armed. There would be no pushing him around.

One day a State seaplane landed on the lake and taxied close to the shore. Two armed men got out on the pontoons and held up legal eviction papers. Nuge said, "When I saw them coming, I went down and sat on the bank of the shore. I put a rifle on one side of me and a pistol on the other." (I remember vividly that Nugent always had a huge .45 caliber revolver nearby—usually in a dark leather holster on his hip whenever he was in the woods.)

"I never touched or raised either one of the guns. But I told them that they were not going to step ashore!" They got the message. After a heated exchange of words, they climbed back aboard the plane and took off. "And they never came back," Nuge said with a merry twinkle in his eye.

In time, word of the Nugents' wilderness enterprise began circulating among the community of wealthy sportsmen, and they began building a clientele. They said even members of the Du Pont family visited. The lure, of course, was the location in that huge, virtually untouched wilderness with its great fishing, hunting, and outdoor recreation. And the Nugents' hospitality and charm.

It eventually became evident to the State that their presence at Chamberlain Lake was an asset. The pair was catering to rich and powerful clients. They also provided a point of safety and means of communication to the growing number of people who were going to the Allagash region: canoeists taking the Allagash River trip, bush pilots, and later, snowmobilers. The state came up with a long-term lease at a nominal cost, and legitimized them.

For over thirty years, Al Nugent ranged the Allagash country, running long, lonely traplines and guiding sportsmen. During the early years he covered many hundreds of miles on snowshoes while carrying heavy traps and supplies on his back, or dragging them on a homemade "moose" sled. Patty often accompanied him.

During the early 1950s, when fur prices soared and a big beaver pelt brought in as much as seventy or eighty dollars for a "blanket" beaver, Nuge learned to fly a ski equipped Piper Cub to monitor his wilderness traplines. This turned out to be full of adventure.

For a time he teamed up with a young fellow pilot and trapper who had an Aeronca Chief, a light plane similar to the Cub but with side-by-side seating instead of the Cub's tandem arrangement. They would fly over the forests in the fall, spotting likely beaver ponds and colonies. Then, when trapping season opened in the winter, they would fly over, drop a pack of traps, and then land on the nearest pond and hike in to set and tend their traps, avoiding long snowshoe treks carrying heavy loads. This worked great, but it had its hazards.

One day they landed on a narrow, twisting pond in their ski-equipped plane. They were skimming along on the snow-covered ice when they rounded a corner and found open water just ahead. They immediately opened full throttle and the plane lifted off just feet from the edge of the ice. (Yes, it's possible to encounter thin ice and open water in even the coldest below-zero weather, due to flowing water currents.)

On another day, just after a winter rain followed by a cold snap, they landed on a pond that was a glare sheet of ice. The wind was blowing sharply and, as they shut down and stepped out, a gust caught the plane and started skidding it down the slippery lake. There was no way to safely get to the propeller to hand-prop the engine. They hung onto the wing struts, their boots sliding ineffectively, as they went sailing merrily down the pond. They feared it would crash into the woods and tear up the fabric airplane, but they finally managed to steer it into the lee of a point and stop it.

Nuge told me that after that experience he hoped to devise a means of utilizing a plane's existing brake system to drive a steel pin down into the ice, but to my knowledge he never did. At least I know of none that exists.

⚜

After a few prosperous seasons, a change in fashion styles scuttled the fur market and made trapping by air economically unfeasible. Nuge again took to the snowshoe trails.

It was about this time that he saw his first over-snow traveling vehicle. It was owned by another wilderness trapper, Forrest Smith, who was operating from Ragged Lake to the southwest of Chamberlain. Smith, another legendary North Woods character, was giving up trapping to devote more time to his specialty: handmade snowshoes.

Nuge, recognizing the advantages of such a machine, lost little time in acquiring one. Although his new snowmobile bore slight resemblance to today's breed, it was a tough work machine. It provided swift transportation on wind-packed lake ice, and it could negotiate snow-covered tote roads and trails previously accessible only to the snowshoer. He found it even beat trapping by air. Nuge could now drive right up to a beaver lodge with a big load of traps aboard.

Nugent's Eliason Motor Toboggan, now on display at the Patten Lumbermen's Museum along with other of his artifacts, was built by the Four Wheel Drive Auto Company of Clintonville, Wisconsin. Nuge said he thought the company began building them around 1920. The company later operated a branch factory at Kitchener, Ontario.

The Eliason machine came equipped with an Indian motorcycle engine rated at 25 horsepower. It had a chain drive made up of motorcycle chains, with cleats to provide traction and flotation on snow. It could do 35 miles per hour in good going, went ten miles on a gallon of gas, and cost $1,800 new.

The development of modern snowmobiles, which began almost simultaneously in the late 1950s by Bombardier in Quebec and Polaris in Minnesota, would have a big impact on the Nugents' business.

I hadn't seen Al and Patty in several years. I was working as a newspaper journalist and magazine writer in the early 1960s when I was invited to go along and document one of the early snowmobile treks to northern Maine. The organizer of the expedition was Bob Morrill, a businessman from Yarmouth, Maine. Allan Hetteen, the president of Polaris Company of Roseau, Minnesota, brought a truckload of new machines of various designs to the state to test them under rigorous conditions, attempting to reap some publicity for his fledgling industry.

The trek in early March covered over two hundred rugged miles in a round-trip from Millinocket through Baxter State Park and across the Allagash headwater lakes to Churchill Dam. The machines were early prototypes. They were heavy, and we were towing sledges loaded with all the supplies needed by a dozen men for ten days. We encountered a lot of deep, soft snow. The result? We spent an awful lot of time and energy digging out and "nudging" stuck snowmobiles and sleds.

On the most brutal day of that journey, we blew into Nugents' seeking shelter. We had broken camp at Churchill Dam that morning and started on our trip back to Millinocket and civilization. It was bitter cold. The temperature was in the low minus-20s, with a gale blowing out of the northwest. It was tolerable crossing the relatively protected ice of Churchill and

Eagle lakes, but the North Pole couldn't have offered conditions much worse than what we found on Chamberlain.

It's about a dozen miles from the Tramway, at the head of Chamberlain, down to Nugent's camps. The lake lies northwest to southeast—a clean, unbroken sweep for the howling wind. It whipped up blinding snow which cut visibility to yards. Most of the time we couldn't see the other machines in the group. Tracks were covered over in seconds. The wind chill must have been near 50-below, and it tore at our army surplus clothing—the best available at the time. People have perished under such conditions.

Somehow, perhaps by instinct, we all made it down the lake and to the warmth and security of Nugent's Wilderness Camps. (Funny how bad weather seemed to dog me in that region.) One whiff of Patty's fresh-baked bread just coming out of the oven of her big wood-burning stove was enough. We elected to wait out the big blow right there. The Nugents took this sudden invasion by a dozen rough guys with welcoming calm.

I wrote up that trip for a newspaper article given wider distribution by the Associated Press, as well as a magazine article. One day a man came into the newspaper office and asked to speak to me.

My first look sized him up as an outdoorsman: tall, rangy, with a weathered face that bespoke much time in the elements. He wore typical outdoor garb—flannel shirt, work pants, boots with patches. I was soon to find out that Harry C. Crooker, belying his appearance, was the most successful contractor in Brunswick. He said, "I read about your trip, and I'd like to go up there with you. I just bought a new snowmobile, and I'm interested in finding old logging equipment."

Soon after, Harry and I were on the way to the Allagash— two guys on one snowmobile, with no backup. No one else in that whole region had a snow machine at the time. Nuge's Eliason Toboggan was already broken down and retired. There were still no roads in that area. Just getting there was an adventure. In my dotage, I sometimes shudder at the risks we took.

This was the first of a number of such trips we made, as we used Nugent's as our base of operations to search for lumbering relics. Picking Nuge's knowledge of the country and locations of old lumber camps, we traveled many miles and never saw another trace of humans.

The gods were obviously looking out for us fools. A serious breakdown or accident would have left us stranded miles from any help, with no means of communication.

Oh, we did have a couple of interesting "incidents." One day we were traveling along the Thoroughfare between Eagle and Churchill lakes. Since this is the outlet of Eagle, it has a flow of current and is dangerous for thin ice. On a foolish whim, we decided to take a shortcut across the Thoroughfare rather than taking the slightly longer way around.

I grabbed the ax off the sled and, as Harry waited at the machine, I started walking across, hitting the ice with the ax to test its strength. I was just about at the middle when suddenly the ax, which had been bouncing off solidly, broke through with a sickening crunch. There was less than a half-inch of ice just inches ahead of my boots! I stood frozen for a moment, and then slowly backed away.

Harry, with his droll humor, said, "Well, if you'd broken through there's nothing I could've done for you. I'd have just driven away!"

We tried to avoid the temptation of "shortcuts" after that incident. But it didn't always work.

We were heading back to camp after one of our forays. It was getting dark, and we were anticipating a warm supper and jovial evening. I was driving.

About four miles north of Nugent's is a long, narrow point that juts out into the lake. This was covered with a hard-packed snow drift, and I elected to drive over it rather than go out around the end of the point.

Wrong move.

The sled flew up the side of the drift, but suddenly the snow softened under us and we bogged down. It seemed like a minor problem, as we'd been stuck in soft snow before.

This was in the days when snowmobiles had side skis; the drive track and engine were hinged at the front and free-floated. It was an ungainly affair which led to many problems and was corrected in subsequent models.

We began digging around the machine, expecting to be under way in minutes. An hour later we were still at it, digging and revving the engine, but it was stuck solidly. Finally we managed to get enough mealy snow cleared away to see the problem. A piece of dri-ki had gone through the track between cleats and locked it up. A few whacks with the ax freed us, and we were on our way to the beckoning lantern lights of camp.

On a later trip to Nugent's we had another misadventure. By now, the Great Northern Paper Company, which owned most of the timberlands in that region, had built a gravel logging road all the way up to the Round Pond Thoroughfare and spanned it with a bridge. We were able to drive that close to camp, easing our journey considerably.

Harry had just purchased a new toy, a Polaris "Bullcat." This was a formidable machine, with a big wide track, powerful engine, and even a cab for side-by-side seating and protection from the weather. We were going in style. Nothing could stop this machine.

Or so we thought.

We drove to the arm of Chamberlain, at the extreme end of the lake and only a few miles from Nugent's camps. We started out in a spray of snow, and had gone barely a mile up the lake when the engine sputtered a few times and died. It took a few minutes to locate the problem. Brushing snow away, we found a minor engineering flaw: The fuel line from tank to carburetor had slipped into the clutch housing, which had worn a big hole in the plastic line.

And, as the old saying goes, "There we were." At least sixty miles from the nearest town and repairs. But again, Lady Luck favored us. We went back to the bridge at the Thoroughfare. A lumbering contractor had a workshop here for their equipment. We entered the garage/workshop. It was the dirtiest, greasiest place I've ever seen. The lone mechanic, a French-Canadian who spoke no English and was black with grease from head to toe, looked at the piece of hose in Harry's hand. Then he pointed to a greasy box under the workbench. We rummaged in the box and found just what we needed. In a few minutes we had the tube repaired and were on our way back to the machine—and another week of exploring the Allagash Region from Nugent's.

All of this occurred before the big wave of snowmobiling popularity soon began invading the Allagash and the Nugents' wilderness Shangri-la. Within a few years, they began doing a bigger business catering to snowmobilers than they'd ever done with the summer sportsmen. Large groups began descending upon them in January, February, and March. Some were drawn by the excellent ice-fishing for trout, but the majority came to explore this big, primitive, beautiful country, and to bask in the warmth of the unique Nugent hospitality.

My excursions to their camps became less frequent. I got busy with other career moves, and somehow the old, homey charm was dulled by the increasing crowds.

Nuge lived well into his seventies, and kept doing what he enjoyed—cutting ice from the lake to fill his icehouse, growing a vegetable garden, guiding sportsmen, and that never-ending task of harvesting firewood. In fact, he died while doing just that. He was hauling firewood to the woodshed when he dropped, apparently dying instantly. I'm sure that's how he would have wanted it.

Patty continued on, running the busy enterprise until her own health began to fade. On a summer day, dozens of her friends, former guests, and ex-employees flew and boated in from places across the country for a "Patty's Day" gathering. This tribute was close to the end for the gallant woodswoman who had stood by her sturdy man through years of adversity and reward.

With the passing of the Nugents, it was feared by many that their camps would be no more. When the state took over the region to create the Allagash Wilderness Waterway, it's reported that an early administrator, who considered the place a "wilderness dump" thanks to Nuge's decades-long collection of lumbering relics which filled a couple of sheds, threatened that as soon as the Nugents were gone he would have the place bulldozed out of existence. He couldn't touch it while they lived there because of a lifetime lease.

Fortunately, wiser heads again prevailed. The bureaucrat was removed, and the camps were leased out to someone who continued to operate them. You can still stay there today.

The last time I was in the region I was on assignment, and a park ranger stopped his boat at the camps on the way by to let me have a look. The shores of Chamberlain still looked much the same, protected from development and lumbering scars by the Allagash Wilderness Park rules. Some of the original cabins have had to be removed due to the ravages of time and weather. They've been replaced by several gleaming new log cabins equipped with modern conveniences. It's still a delightful place, although the old Nugent lifestyle and unique ambiance are gone.

You can see some of Nuge's stuff, including the Eliason Motor Toboggan, by making a visit to the Lumbermen's Museum at Patten on the road to the northern entrance to Baxter State Park. Here the Nugents' legacy lives on.

As Nuge would say: "Jest right!"

23

Crystal Harvest

When Ice Was Gold

ACROSS AN EXPANSE OF FROZEN LAKE SURFACE, several burly, bright-garbed men are at work cutting ice with handsaws and chisels. In the background, the wild, forested shore crowds up to a small cluster of log cabins with snow-covered roofs. Smoke plumes curl from the chimneys. It's a picture-perfect scene, something from Currier & Ives.

At one time this was a common winter sight throughout the frozen North. It's still found only in a few isolated places far removed from the power grid, places like the Bradford Camps on Munsungan Lake, Matt Libby's Camps on Millinocket Lake, and Gary Cobb's Pierce Pond Camps. All are sporting camps located in remote wilderness areas of northern Maine.

At Bradford Camps, they still put up an average of twelve tons every January, according to Igor Sikorsky III. "We try for the early season, because we have better ice then, and it's not too thick. A nine- to twelve-inch layer of clear ice is our ideal. We cut blocks about twelve-inch square which gives us fifty- to eighty-pound blocks, depending on depth."

Sikorsky has a team of ten experienced guys who have been ice-cutting together for years. They've developed their team-work, and turn the once-a-year chore into practically a game. "With two cutters, two yankers, two loaders, two sledders, a gantry [hoist] person, and two people in the icehouse, we can get the work done in about four hours—or beer equivalent, which is about six. Ten guys is just the right amount."

They've even developed their own language. They are the FSS, or "Free Shoveling Society," as the group has to shovel the snow off an approximately fifty-by-fifty-foot area to expose the ice. "Chuck" is the area of ice needed to fill the icehouse. "Frank" is an ice block that shatters, making it undesirable for storage. "Bark" is the process of cutting a bar of ice into cakes. And an "icehouse troll" is the guy at the end of the day who has spent the last four hours inside, stooped over, picking up sixty-pound blocks, as he comes out squinting and bent into the daylight.

Here's their more cerebral phrase: "We take pride in our cubism." And finally, there's the "dividend," which is "the hidden can of beer we stuff in the ice to await the spring when some lucky soul finds it. The most perfectly chilled beer in the world."

Each sporting camp has developed a system for cutting, hauling, and storing the ice. At Cobb's, owner Gary (and his father before him) has been "putting up" ice for his summer camp guests for over a half-century. On a crisp February weekend, Gary, his son Andy, and a crew of ten hardy employees and volunteers spend a work-crammed weekend cutting blocks out of the nearly two-foot-thick ice in the lake in front of the camps. The toilers experience toe-freezing and nose-biting cold, but next summer's camp guests will be able to enjoy iced

Photo courtesy Gary Cobb collection

Ice harvesting at Cobb's Pierce Pond Camps Lodge and guest cabins in background. Crew of ten harvests ten tons of pure lake ice each February.

drinks and pack their lunch in ice-cooled containers. And the winter ice will augment the camp kitchen's gas-powered, walk-in refrigerator.

Years ago Cobb bought an antique ice-cutting machine from the Titcomb family of Abbott, Maine. The ungainly looking contraption is mounted on rugged sled runners, and it still uses a 1929 Model A Ford engine, geared to turn a large circular saw. Gary said the engine, not started since last year's cut, "fires and roars to life on the first try. Not to worry. Mr. Ford made a great engine back in the Roaring Twenties!"

It takes most of the ten-man crew to haul and push the saw rig over the ice to "mark" the field, cutting down into the surface ice several inches to create strips that are fourteen inches wide. Then comes the hard work. Using the antique handsaws developed over a century ago, the guys cut along the strips to release the ice's grip. This is a push-pull, up-and-down labor that soon exhausts even the hardiest.

Then the strips are broken into precise, fourteen-inch-square blocks by cutting them apart with a "busting bar"—a toothed iron chisel with a wide blade. Even Igor Sikorsky, having already finished putting up the ice at Munsungan, shows up to help his old friends, the Cobbs.

Since each cake weighs an estimated 180 to 220 pounds depending on the thickness of the ice, Gary has devised a "galamander." This is a tall wooden tripod holding a rope. A pair of tongs is hooked into each ice block, which is then hoisted above the lake surface and loaded aboard a sledge to be brought to the old, log icehouse, which can hold ten tons of ice. Here it is carefully packed with snow and sawdust, which will preserve its frozen state into the sweltering summer.

As the crew cuts ice, Gary's wife Betty is busy in the camp kitchen, making hot soup and a variety of other hot dishes and desserts to feed the hungry group as they drop in to thaw and refuel.

Gary notes: "It's beautiful ice. It's a soft blue, and so clear you can almost see through it."

At Libby's Camps, the ice-cutting ritual has a festive feel. They coincide it with Martin Luther King weekend, says Matt Libby, and up to twenty friends show up. Some turn it into a full week to enjoy snowmobiling, ice-fishing, and winter camp life.

According to Matt, their equipment includes "an old 80cc Husqvarna saw with an Alaska sawmill attachment, a rope, a guide for marking the ice, ice chisel, ice tongs, snowmobile,

and snow sled. We provide the grub and the ibuprofen." The
ice is stored in a log house built of cedar and insulated with
sawdust.

Curiosity and nostalgia brought me to Nugent's Camps
on Chamberlain Lake in the Allagash Wilderness Region to
observe the annual ice-cutting ritual some years ago.

Patty and Allen Nugent accommodated fishermen and
campers in that wild country for nearly half a century. Nugent's
Camps, still operating under that name but under new management since the passing of the founders, is located over fifty
miles from the nearest town and electric power lines.

Back in their day, the Nugents cut their own ice each winter
and stored it inside an icehouse, which Nuge had built himself
from hand-hewn logs, with hand-split cedar shakes for the roof.
The thick log walls and aromatic sawdust served to insulate the
ice.

The morning of my visit dawned sparkling-bright with frost.
Fortified with one of Patty Nugent's lumberjack breakfasts, we
gathered on the Chamberlain ice to observe Nuge and his crew
at work.

Al Nugent was a man of legendary size and strength. In
his early years at Chamberlain he did the entire ice-cutting
job alone, spending weeks at the harsh labor. "I'd saw out the
cakes, load 'em on a moose sled, and haul 'em by hand up t' the
icehouse," he explained.

We heard someone tell a story of his great strength. Several ice fishermen had gathered around to watch Nuge at
work. Each tried his strength at lifting one big cake from the
water, and each failed. One of them bet Al that he couldn't
single-handedly lift the cake a foot clear of the ground. Nuge
took the challenge, spat on his hands, grabbed the ice tongs,

grinned—and hoisted the cake high, almost trotting with it all the way up to the icehouse without setting it down once to rest.

⸺⸺✕⸺⸺

For a generation that's grown up with frozen food, life without the miracle of electric refrigerators might seem intolerable. Yet this staple of modern-day convenience has been available for only a relatively few decades.

For much of humankind's history, perishable food had to be consumed almost immediately, or preserved with crude drying and salting, often poor substitutes for wholesome freshness. Spices came into use not merely for piquing the taste buds but also to conceal the taste of advanced ripening in foods.

In those "good old days," many people could not cool their drinks, families had few reliable means of preserving their perishable foods, and children didn't know the ecstasy of an ice-cream cone on a sweltering day.

But while the tropics sizzled, residents of the northern latitudes had an abundance of a natural preservative: winter ice. It didn't take long for Yankee ingenuity to uncover its business potential.

From the early 1800s into the 1920s, northern ice began to revolutionize man's centuries-old ways of living.

Summer relief for much of the world's parched cities began arriving in the form of windjammers laden with this magical ice from the northeastern United States. There was already a sizable fleet of these ships, though the era of wooden sailing vessels was nearing its demise, succumbing to the power of steam. Yankee skippers sailed the globe, peddling a crystal treasure from their homeland of green forests and clean, pure lakes and rivers. Many harvested great wealth from this free "crop," provided by nature in bounteous quantity each winter.

While Texans drilled for oil and Californians dug for yellow nuggets of gold, New Englanders harvested the diamond crystals that formed on rivers and lakes. Millions of tons of ice were shipped to all parts of the Earth, including India, South America, and Europe. Rail lines hauled hundreds of thousands of tons to the interior states of North America.

Ice speculation ran rampant. Huge fortunes were gambled, made, or lost on the whims of nature and her cold north winds. Those engaged in it boasted that it was a business that wouldn't be replaced. (Take heed, ye planners of the twenty-first century.)

During the heyday of King Ice, the tidewater area of Maine's Kennebec River was the world's center for the booming industry. Other northeastern lakes and rivers also produced ice in phenomenal amounts.

Most of the New York ice came from the Hudson above Newburgh, and from lakes near the river. In the early 1870s, it was reported that the annual ice harvest in the Hudson Valley supplying New York City and Brooklyn was 1,160,000 tons. Demand there was increasing at the rate of about 70,000 tons per year.

But the then-pure Kennebec River waters flowing down from Moosehead Lake and its surrounding northern forests, coupled with a rugged winter climate, made it the queen of ice rivers. During the 1890s, the average Kennebec ice harvest exceeded three million tons annually. It was worth over $36 million.

The ice boom employed thousands of able-bodied men. These were primarily farmers and hired hands from the

229

numerous small farms dotting the river valleys. But many itinerant laborers and even hoboes, drawn by the lure of fifteen-cent-an-hour wages and the hearty food and warm beds of riverside boardinghouses, took part.

On those bright, brittle winter days, swarms of men and horses blackened the ice surface as they scraped away the snow, grooved the ice with horse-drawn markers into huge checkerboards, sawed off long strips of the surface, and broke the individual cakes with heavy iron chisels. Using long poles tipped with steel picks and hooks, other men steered the ice cakes into canals cut through the ice to steam-powered chain-link conveyers. These lifted the heavy cakes into huge icehouses, many larger than football fields, lining the riverbank. These houses had double walls stuffed with sawdust for insulation.

When the houses were full, they were covered with insulating sawdust or hay to await the arrival of spring. In peak years the cakes overflowed the houses and the surplus piled into huge stacks on the riverbank.

Spring meant ice-out. The first ships began making their way past Fort Popham at the mouth of the Kennebec and beating up the river past the city of Bath, through Merrymeeting Bay, and almost to Augusta, nearly fifty miles inland, where the river's banks were lined with wharves and icehouses.

What better harbinger of spring than these tall-masted schooners, most of them Maine-built? The aging ships were swiftly loaded, and they caught the earliest favorable tide downriver to faraway ports. These wooden ships hauling ice marked an end of the two-century-old reign of Yankee shipbuilders and world tradesmen, once steam-powered ships took their place.

But it was those Yankee skippers and their graceful vessels who brought the magic crystals of Maine winters to the exotic regions of the world—to sting the fingers and light rapture in the eyes of youngsters who had never seen the wonder of ice flakes until they chased the iceman's wagon and stole chips that fell from his pick.

Soon came the modern miracles of electricity and internal combustion. The age of the tall-masted sailing craft ended. The ice industry waned and died almost coincidentally with the rise of industrial development and its consequent water pollution. The ice rivers of the industrial North turned dirty, the ice unsafe for human use.

Wooden schooners rotted, a process accelerated by the freshwater from melting ice in their holds, and sank at their moorings. Huge, neglected icehouses began to leak, tilt, and collapse, their roofs no longer able to hold the crushing burdens of winter snows.

The ice harvesters and their horses turned their backs to the rivers and entered the forests to cut the pulpwood required to feed the paper mills, which in turn were poisoning the once-pure rivers with their noxious effluents.

The tools used in the ice industry were re-forged by thrifty Down East farmers into new implements for woods work. Or they were sold as junk. Or they merely rusted away in old barns or farm dumps. A few have been preserved in museums, and some remain at a few Maine wilderness camps, where they still serve their purpose.

Icemen and iceboxes persisted in small towns and villages until the late 1930s. As a very young child, I remember seeing the horse-drawn ice wagon, pulled by a large, gentle chestnut, working the streets of my hometown of Chisholm, Maine. Later, the horse and wagon were replaced by a more-efficient but less-picturesque stake-body truck.

When I got big enough, I sometimes joined neighborhood boys in chasing after the truck to "steal" chips from its tailgate, while the driver purposely looked the other way. He'd made sure extra chips were lying on the tailgate for us.

Refrigerators were available at the stores, but not many families could afford that luxury in those days of the Great Depression. The iceman would cruise the streets, checking the windows. Each ice customer had been issued a special card. Numbers—10¢, 25¢, 50¢, 75¢—would designate the size ice cake you wanted that day. The customer would turn the card so that the appropriate number was at the bottom.

The biggest cakes were the ones you purchased to carry you over the weekend in the dog days of summer. The iceman, always a big, burly guy with bulging muscles, would pick up the big ice block with tongs and carry it into the house and place it in the icebox. Sometimes he'd climb up three or four flights of stairs in tall apartment buildings. And just as with today's postman, there were jokes aplenty about the remarkable resemblance of a family's kids to the iceman.

On hot weekends my dad would drop chunks of ice into a burlap bag and use the back of his ax to crush the ice into smaller pieces. These were then dumped, along with some rock salt, into the ice-cream maker, which contained the ingredients Mom had already prepared. We bigger boys fought to turn the hand crank for the seemingly interminable length of time it took for the mixture to turn hard, indicating the ice cream was finished. Then the luckiest kid, if not the biggest, got the chance to lick the frozen cream off the paddle. It was so cold your tongue sometimes stuck to it. Nothing since has ever tasted as good.

In tiny South Bristol, near the Damariscotta River in coastal Maine, the Thompson Ice House is one of the last places where you can still see ice harvesting—not as a sterile exhibit, but in real life. This is a "living museum"; no virtual reality here.

It began in 1826 when Asa Thompson dammed a brook to create the ice pond and built the icehouse. The business continued through five generations of Thompsons, until Herbert Thompson closed it in 1969. Kenneth Lincoln, who began working for the Thompsons at age ten, organized the museum in 1990. Lincoln leads a group of volunteers each winter in harvesting the ice using the Thompsons' old tools.

Each year they fill the icehouse and relive history—even to the point of sometimes using a pair of draft horses and hoist to raise the heavy cakes up into the building. During the summer the museum sells ice to local residents, just as in the old days. And they top it off with an old-fashioned ice-cream social each July, with ice cream churned by hand by "cranky old men."

Harvesting and storing natural ice, part of the simple (some would say primitive) way of life for people like the Nugents and the Thompsons, was common among many Americans only a few decades ago. In this day of urban sprawl and energy challenges, many of us may well envy that waning lifestyle, with its uncomplicated security and self-dependence.

A version of this story appeared in the February
2013 issue of *Down East* magazine.